A Wholly Life

A Wholly Life
Spiritual Integration of Mind, Body, and Soul

Compiled by Moshe Kaplan, MD

TARGUM/FELDHEIM

First published 2005
Copyright © 2005 by Moshe Kaplan
ISBN 1-56871-375-4

Published by:
TARGUM PRESS, INC.
22700 W. Eleven Mile Rd.
Southfield, MI 48034
E-mail: targum@netvision.net.il
Fax: 888-298-9992
www.targum.com

Distributed by:
FELDHEIM PUBLISHERS
208 Airport Executive Park
Nanuet, NY 10954

Printing plates by Frank, Jerusalem
Printed in Israel by Chish

בית פינחס

בן אדמו"ר מסטמאר שליט"א
הרב לוי יצחק הלוי הורוויץ
ניחין ירושלים חלי
Grand Rabbi Levi I. Horowitz
The Bostoner Rebbe

Spirituality is many things to many people. For too many, spirituality is an escape from living — from family, friends, and community, from caring for physical health, from developing an intellectual understanding of the world and one's place in it. Judaism teaches an inclusive spirituality that transforms every area of "normal" life. Jewish spirituality teaches committed Jews how to live spiritually together with their families, friends, and communities. Jewish spirituality elevates work and social responsibility to holy pursuits. Jewish spirituality enables the intellect to become a means to spiritualizing the whole person. And Jewish spirituality is concerned with physical health as well. All of life is transformed when the Creator is perceived as present in all of life. Our goal is to live in a conscious relationship with Him. Jewish spirituality is reaching this goal.

A Wholly Life: Spiritual Integration of Mind, Body, and Soul is a portrait of the many faces of Jewish spirituality. It brings together contributions by people who have elevated their secular expertise to the service of the spiritual. Philosophers, physical scientists, psychologists, physical trainers, doctors, and rabbis will find colleagues here. The reader will gain a vision of how every aspect of life can be elevated into a spiritual pursuit. Dr. Moshe Kaplan is to be commended for having provided an authentic vision of Jewish spirituality in practice. We pray that the book will lead many to explore the Jewish teaching of spirituality further and inspire them to apply its lessons to their lives.

DEDICATION

This book is dedicated to the memory of HaGaon HaRav Chaim Kreisworth, *zt"l*. Praised and loved by all who knew him, his brilliance, warmth, and deliberate, polite, and modest good character inspired a generation.

It was a gift to be close to such a saintly soul.

PREFACE

Many of the ideas recorded in this book were first presented to me by my own teachers; others I found in various sources. Generally speaking, I do not quote directly from those sources. Let me, though, make it clear at the outset that many of the ideas expressed in this book are not originally mine, but are drawn from classical Jewish thought.

I wish to thank God for the inspiration to compile this book. I also wish to express thanks to all the distinguished authorities who reviewed this book and made apt and instructive comments.

Moshe Kaplan

Contents

Joseph Lieberman received his law degree from Yale Law School. He is currently the United States Senator from the State of Connecticut.

Senator Joseph Lieberman

PROLOGUE

I always say that from the first moment of my life I was fortunate because of the two parents I was lucky enough to be born to. They gave me many gifts, and especially two gifts of faith.

The first was "faith" in its most literal meaning, faith in God and in a tradition that had come down through the ages. The rabbis that I was privileged to grow up studying with helped me to answer the questions that everyone has: Who am I? And what am I doing here? And they have continued, through all the opportunities I've had, to give order and purpose and direction to my life. The busier I've gotten in public life, the more I've appreciated and even depended on the path that my parents put me on, including in particular Sabbath observance.

Sometimes people will say to me, how can you be involved as a United States Senator and find time to observe the Sabbath? And my answer, honestly, quite sincerely, is I don't know how I could do this without observing the Sabbath. Because, you know, part of it is just plain physical, and in some ways psychological, that you can work extra hard on those other days knowing that — as a wonderful bumper sticker that I once saw said — Relax, the Sabbath is coming. And there is something to that. So my parents gave me that faith.

The other "faith" they gave me was a faith in America. My parents said to me, this country is so great that you don't have to hide who you are to be a good American. You don't have to homogenize yourself because the greatness of this country is that it invites you to be who you are — whether it's your religion, your nationality, obviously your race, or your ethnicity — and in that diversity America gains its strength. We are an unusual nation, defined not so much by a set order as by a set of ideals. Freedom, opportunity, and tolerance are central to those ideals.

I must say that I am so grateful for all of this that, in the spirit of giving back, in the spirit and the ethical tradition of our religion, I do feel a special obligation in the years ahead of me in public service to do whatever I can to make sure that every child in this country, every girl or boy born to anyone in this country, can have the dream that they can grow up to be Vice President of the United States.

When you look at our history I think the framers had the insight that in a democracy, where the government will not be telling everybody what to do at every moment, where there will not be dictatorial control, to have a good society people need other sources of values. And the values that come from religion, from the Torah, from the Old Testament, are exactly those kinds of values.

If you look at the history of America, some of the critical moments of progress that have occurred have been stimulated by religious movements. The Abolitionist Movement in the eighteenth century began in religious groups. In the late nineteenth and early twentieth century, it was again religious groups that stimulated the wave of social welfare legislation and the worker protection and child labor protection legislation. And of course, closer to our time, it was a group of broad-based religious leaders who stimulated the modern-day Civil Rights Movement that has affected all of us.

The good fortune I had in being selected to run for Vice President did not occur in a vacuum. I was not just plucked out of the stream of history to have this extraordinary privilege, but I stood, as the old saying goes, on the shoulders of so many who had gone before me. I am grateful to the generations of Jewish Americans who preceded me — and not just those in public life, but in business and in the professions, in philanthropy and community leaders — all those who have increasingly played such a large and honorable and constructive role in American life.

*After completing his medical training in the US, **Dr. Moshe Kaplan** practiced psychoimmunology in California for a few years. He then moved to Israel where he started his career as an investment banker, utilizing his medical skills for charitable purposes. He now lives in Jerusalem, where he writes and works on his God connection.*

Dr. Moshe Kaplan

INTRODUCTION

If the statistics are right, the Jews constitute but one percent of the human race... Properly, the Jew ought hardly to be heard of...but he is as prominent on the planet as any other people... The Jew saw [the Egyptians, Babylonians, Persians, Greeks and Romans], beat them all, and is now what he always was... All things are mortal but the Jew; all other forces pass, but he remains. What is the secret of his immortality?

Mark Twain

The Jew is that sacred being who has brought down from heaven the everlasting fire, and has illumined with it the entire world. He is the religious source, spring, and fountain out of which all the rest of the peoples have drawn their beliefs and their religions. The Jew is the pioneer of liberty. The Jew is the pioneer of civilization. The Jew is the emblem of eternity.

Leo Tolstoy

The Jews have done more to civilize men than any other nation... They are the most glorious nation that ever inhabited the earth. The Romans and their empire were but a bauble in comparison to the Jews. They have given religion to three-quarters of the globe and have influenced the affairs of mankind more, and more happily, than any other nation, ancient or modern.

John Adams
(second president of the United States)

The secret of the Jews' immortality is our relationship with the Divine. We are each to sanctify ourselves and make ourselves holy — and by so doing be partners with God in building the world. This is the charge implied in the famous verse, "As for the heavens, the heavens are God's, but the earth He has given to mankind" (Psalms 115).

Turnus Rufus the Wicked once asked Rabbi Akiva: "Whose works are better, the works of God or the works of human beings?"

Rabbi Akiva answered, "The works of human beings…"

Rufus then asked him, "Why do you circumcise?"

Rabbi Akiva replied, "I knew that you were asking about this. That is why I anticipated your question by saying that the works of human beings are better."

Turnus Rufus objected, "But if God wanted man to be circumcised, why didn't He arrange for boys to be born that way?"

Rabbi Akiva answered, "Because the Holy One, Blessed is He, gave the commandments to Israel so we could be purified through them."

(*Midrash Tanchuma, Tazria* 5)

God's gift to humankind, created in the Divine image, is the existence of spirituality beyond physicality. Besides impurity and death there is also the possibility of purity and eternal life.

We have the power to overcome our physical impediments and imperfections. We can ennoble and sanctify our animal drives and instincts. By doing so, we perfect human nature and redeem an imperfect world, for the route to a life of sanctity requires making sacred the materialistic and mundane around us.

Rav Yerucham Levovitz, *zt"l, mashgiach* of the Mir Yeshiva, explains:

> Whereas all other living things are created essentially in a state of completion and need only to grow in size and mass, man is created as raw potential and must invest a great deal of effort to become what he was meant to be. A human being's goal is to strive toward perfection, knowing it can never be achieved. This is man's mission.

God created the world to bestow His kindness upon us. This world is beautiful and magnificent, but it nevertheless needs completion and perfection. This is accomplished, first and foremost, by our strengthening our weaknesses, repairing our transgressions, and sublimating our drives to sanctify God's creation. Each defect in the acts of individual people ultimately impacts on the entire universe.

We are given free moral choice, but we have responsibility. Just as a passenger in a boat cannot drill a hole under his seat and tell others to mind their own business, so we cannot say that our actions only affect us individually. We have an obligation to strive for wholeness, balancing and harmonizing our needs with the needs of our neighbors, friends, and loved ones — contradictions and all.

When a person enters the world he becomes a hired watchman for his body and soul and, as an adult, is responsible for all his behavior except for unusual events beyond his control. Fulfilling that responsibility by perfecting his behavior is what makes a person holy.

This is not a simple charge, nor is the best route to achieve it always obvious. However, many people have made the journey and can offer us their experience if we seek it. Some of those experiences are joyous, some trials, but all provide insight in how to achieve true sanctity rather than an illusion.

In our own lives, we must view our own joys and trials through the lens of trust in our Maker. We must understand that ultimately everything under His aegis (meaning absolutely everything!) is for the good — and use the experiences with which He provides us to sanctify ourselves and the world. In so doing, we will accomplish much more than a private communion with God. Just as an organism only functions well when all its parts are whole and healthy, so does the world only function optimally when all its players act according to the Divine law. Playing by His rules will allow everyone's goals to be achieved. Trying to "beat the system" will eventually run everyone into the ground.

Inasmuch as Jews were made a separate nation for the sole purpose of increasing God's glory in the world (otherwise they could have been left in Egypt), any action that does not contribute toward that goal is misplaced. Not that Jews lack value as individuals, but their value is not that of an island, but rather of a flower in a flower garden — beautiful by itself, but also part of the garden.

As an example, one who takes pleasure from the world without acknowledging the Creator properly is said to be stealing from both God and the Jewish people. By misusing the world, one distances God from His people, and thus essentially robs both of their relationship. For God is driven, so to speak, from a world that could have been holy. Thus, an individual who abandons his responsibilities as a member of the people that can make God's presence manifest has done damage to the entire nation's purpose for existence.

Judaism is not just a religion, it is a way of life. It is meant to be lived on the road, at work, at the gym, ball game, and table. Different people with their different strengths and weaknesses can more easily sanctify different aspects of life, but all are obligated to work toward holiness in every area. Judaism understands God to measure people by how hard they try, not by what they accomplish — but in spiritual matters all are obligated to try! Saintliness is not expected only of some "chosen few." We must all aim for it, because we all have the potential to attain it in some measure.

Many religious systems disdain the physical and preach that the soul triumphs through denial. They believe that physical pleasure seduces a person away from spirituality. This is not the Jewish point of view. Used properly, the physical becomes an invaluable and indispensable aid in the acquisition of spiritual greatness. Our job is to take the worldly gifts that God gives us and elevate them to the heights of holiness — to combine the physical with the spiritual. Physical pleasure finds its place as a subject for gratitude to the One who created physical enjoyment. However, the misuse of physical pleasure has led to all of humanity's struggles, suffering, and unrest. What is needed is the proper fusing of license and restraint, to elevate us and create harmony, serenity, gladness, and joy — holy goals.

Pleasure is holy and pure when it is measured, when the supervising intellect ensures against both excess and denial, and provides the proper intent. Overindulgence in any area of one's physical life, even in the most kosher activity, becomes spiritually destructive. The challenge, then, is to free ourselves of the domination of selfish and self-destructive desires and make room for our longing for the Divine.

How are we to know the proper balance in matters of physical pleasure? For many, common sense is sufficient. For others, help can be found in the traditional sources, such as Rambam, or from a mentor. In any case, both excessive indulgence and excessive self-deprivation must be guarded against. We are called to account in Heaven, it is told, for those things we could have legitimately enjoyed and didn't. The sages of the Talmud say it is no feat to remain pure by fasting and retiring from the world. The real accomplishment is to live in the world, doing what is permitted and avoiding what is prohibited. Judaism is not a life lived only for bold moments and heroic feats. Rather it values and nurtures the everyday details that bring one closer to God's light.

So there is the challenge, given by God to those who choose to take it up. But it is not an even choice. On the one side is sanctity and life. On the other, spiritual death. Nor is it possible not to choose. Choosing not to move forward toward holiness inevitably pushes a person toward a wasteland of spiritual destruction.

Becoming an integrated, holy person requires sanctifying every aspect of one's personal behavior using all of one's God-given abilities and resources. According to one's success in this endeavor, so will he be judged, in this world and in Heaven. As it says in *Avot*:

> Who has wisdom? He who learns from everyone.
> Who has strength? He who conquers temptation.
> Who has wealth? He who is content with his lot.
> Who has honor? He who respects others.

In the end, one's worth is determined by one's character and spiritual achievements.

The Maharal explains that the years of a person's life are like a spiral — we pass over the same ground each year, but move higher with each cycle. A wise person knows that life is a gift that can be utilized well or badly, and that it is never too late to change for the better. Every minute that we are alive there is hope.

As *Avot* further states: "You are not expected to complete your work, but neither are you free to abandon it."

It is my hope that this book will give you a start on the how and why of being God's partner in the creation of the world and ourselves.

Rabbi Dr. Dovid Gottlieb

INTELLECTUAL INTEGRATION

Dr. Dovid Gottlieb *received his PhD in mathematical logic from Brandeis University before teaching philosophy at John Hopkins University. He has published Ontological Economy, Oxford U. Press, 1980; and The Informed Soul, Artscroll, 1990. He received a National Science Foundation Research Grant and published several papers, listed below, before moving to Jerusalem with his family to teach at Ohr Somayach Rabbinical College.*

A partial list of published papers:
1. *"Foundation of Logical Theory,"* American Philosophical Quarterly, *11 (1974), pp. 337–43.*
2. *"Reference and Ontology,"* Journal of Philosophy, *17 (1974), pp. 587–99.*
3. *"A Method for Ontology, with Applications to Numbers and Events,"* Journal of Philosophy, *73 (1976), pp. 637–51.*
4. *"The Truth About Arithmetic,"* American Philosophical Quarterly, *15 (1978), pp. 81–90.*
5. *(With Timothy McCarthy) "Substitutional Quantification and Set Theory,"* Journal of Philosophical Logic, *1979.*

INTRODUCTION

Animals grow and develop until they reach physical maturity. Thereafter, they do only what is necessary to survive, without any other significant growth. Humans, on the other hand, though they stop growing physically when they reach adulthood, can continue to grow intellectually and spiritually throughout their lives. If humans neglect their intellectual and spiritual growth and indulge only in physical needs and desires, their humanity is compromised; only their animal aspect expresses itself. That is why self-respecting, rational people are preoccupied with intellectual and spiritual growth.

How can our intellect help us to grow spiritually? We can look to the experience of the lobster for our answer. The lobster has a soft body and a rigid shell. The shell cannot expand as the lobster grows, so when it grows too large, it sheds its shell and grows a new one. It does this periodically throughout its life. The discomfort of being compressed is a signal to the lobster to dispose of its constraining shell in favor of freer function and continued growth.

So too with us. Intellectual and spiritual distress can mean that, like the lobster, we're ready to grow, but something's holding us back. We need to push aside any obstacles that are blocking our growth. Our intellect acts as a trailblazer and light-bearer for our souls. The mind seeks out, is naturally drawn towards, and absorbs new ideas and concepts, which it then brings back to the soul for approval. "Will this new information help us grow and become closer to God?"

The mind and soul can sense when a new level is ready to be traversed. Judaism helps us to hone our instincts, and the Torah provides a wealth of ideas and information that are each individually designed to enhance the soul. The intimate connection between the mind and soul is instinctive and essential to any person seeking to grow spiritually.

Dr. Dovid Gottlieb, in his essay "A Spiritual Mind," explores this connection.

Rabbi Dr. Dovid Gottlieb

A SPIRITUAL MIND

Once there was a disciple who felt he was not making any spiritual progress. His master told him to go to a certain spot in the forest early in the morning, climb a tree, and wait. The next morning he was there. The day wore on, past noon, nothing. In the middle of the afternoon he heard someone tramping through the forest. He saw it was the town water carrier with his empty barrels on a pole across his shoulders. The water carrier looked around but did not see the disciple in the tree. He then filled the barrels from a nearby stream, put them on the pole over his shoulders, and jumped across the stream. He continued jumping across and back until he fell exhausted on the bank.

The disciple knew that this was what he was supposed to see, but he did not understand. So he climbed down from the tree and addressed the water carrier. "My master sent me here to watch you, but I do not understand what I saw. Please explain what you were doing."

He answered, "I am a simple water carrier. I never

learned to study. But I am strong. I finish my work early.
Then I come to the forest, fill the barrels with water, and
dance in honor of my Creator. He gave me great
muscles, so I use them to celebrate Him."

The water carrier used what he had, the very gifts Hashem
had given him, in order to honor God.

An intellectual person, one who "thinks" the world into an
understandable order, and a spiritual person, who "feels" the
world according to the harmony in his core, seem so different
from one another. It's hard to imagine that one person can be
both. But, as the disciple understood, every part of a person
can contribute to his spirituality — including the intellect.
How does it work?

What Is Spirituality?

Meditating on a mountaintop? Working with the poor?
Studying mystical writings? Which is it?

It's all of these things, for some — and none, for others.
Each culture has a different way of organizing life, differing
ultimate goals, divergent pictures of the way the world "really" is. It's completely subjective, so how is it possible to de-
fine it?

Levi was a poor Jew living in a shtetl in Poland. He had a
dream where he saw himself in Vienna by a bridge. He
dug beside the foundation of the bridge and uncovered a
buried treasure. In the morning he dismissed it as "just"
a dream, but it repeated itself the next night and the next
and the next. Finally, he realized he would have to go to
Vienna.

So he did. He soon found precisely the bridge he had
seen in his dream. But there was a soldier guarding the

bridge. He waited for the moment when the soldier was distracted, and he started to dig.

After only a couple of minutes, he felt a heavy hand on his shoulder. "What are you doing, Jew?" Too frightened to think of a lie, he told the soldier the truth: he was following his dream. The soldier laughed. "You foolish Jews! I too had a dream. I saw a miserable Jew just like you. His name was Levi, and he lived in a shtetl in Poland. Under his oven I saw a buried treasure. Now am I running off to Poland to find a treasure? Get out of here!"

Levi got the message, and he went home and dug up the treasure under his own oven!

So let's start at home and dig up our own treasure. What do 3,800 years of Judaism have to teach us about spirituality? There is more to the world than we see. The entire world, the visible and the invisible, expresses the will of God. God gives everything its being and its life. The purpose of life is to live together with God in a joyous, conscious relationship.

There is more to the world than we see. We know it's true for science: we don't see atoms or gravity or the radio waves that are passing through us all the time. We see what they do — their effects — but we can't actually see them.

The entire world, the visible and the invisible, expresses the will of God. There are layers upon layers. The world did not create itself, and it did not happen by accident. It was created, and is continually in the process of being created. Moment by moment, the will of God gives the world its existence. God usually hides behind the appearance of nature, so the will behind creation is usually not visible. But we can see its effects. In fact, everything we see is its effects!

God gives everything its being and its life. Nothing is by accident. Everything is consciously created and directed to a goal, down to the tiniest detail. Nothing is useless or trivial. Each thing plays its own role in achieving the goal of the whole creation.

The purpose of life is to live together with God in a joyous, conscious relationship. We share certain attributes with God. He expresses consciousness, and we are conscious. God expresses purpose, and we too have purpose. God expresses love, care, commitment, and justice, and we too are capable of expressing these things. Even though we can't see or hear God, we can have a real and profound relationship with Him through the way that He, and we, express our personalities.

Built into the creation of the world are pathways God created for us to relate to Him. Our relationship with Him is in no way arbitrary or ambivalent. It is like relating to a table. Wishing the table was made of gold, or that I could lift it with one finger, won't help. If it isn't, and I can't, then it isn't and I can't. If we retreat into fantasy and just imagine a relationship, we are left with only fantasy. It has to be reciprocal, two-way.

Victor Frankl describes a dying person whose last days were eased by conversing with the tree outside the window. The fact that the "conversation" was imaginary does not reduce its "spirituality" for Frankl.

This kind of fantasy ignores a basic truth: We all want to live in the real world.

Suppose you are offered a special opportunity. Someone has invented a machine that causes dreams. He will program the machine to give you any dreams you want, free of charge. The only catch is that once you are attached to the machine, you go on a life-support system and you remain attached to the machine until you die. Would you take it?

Most people wouldn't. But why not? After all, the dream will be much more pleasant, much more exciting and satisfying than real life would be. But it wouldn't be real! That's enough of a reason for most people to say no.

For the minority who wouldn't care about that, and would pick the dream world, let's take the argument one step further. Let's say you knew how to cure cancer, and you now get the offer to hook up to the machine so you will dream that you are curing cancer. You wouldn't choose the machine because then nobody would really be cured from cancer. Even you would choose the real world under such circumstances.

There are many things we want integrated into our lives: pleasure, excitement, satisfaction. But ultimately, we crave reality, which is the starting point of Jewish spirituality.

Appreciating the Source

Intellectual reality starts with appreciating the intellect as a gift.

You are trying to solve a problem, any kind of problem — how to vote in the elections, how to improve your relationship with someone close to you, how to improve your efficiency in your work, or how to control your anger. How do you go about finding a solution?

You think about it. You discuss it with others, read about it, check the Internet... Suppose nothing helps. What do you do now? You might give up, but you might not. You might think about it again. Maybe something will occur to you this time around. Suppose again you come up with nothing. Then you might let it go for a while — sleep on it overnight or put it out of your mind for a week. Then you think about it again. We have all been through this. Sometimes the problem stays with us for a long period of time. We think about it often and repeat the same thought pattern many times because we've run out of new ideas. And then, suddenly, something new occurs to us. A bolt out of the blue. "Aha — that's it!"

Now where did the solution come from? When we've gone through the same thought pattern that came up empty last time, why did we get the answer this time? Of course, we are all familiar with this. We have all experienced it. "It just happens."

But it doesn't "just happen." Nothing "just happens." Even the scientists agree there has to be some concrete explanation: the unconscious, the influence of changing emotions on the same thought process, the chemical balance in the brain. No definitive conclusions have been reached.

If you have a spiritual focus, then you experience it as a gift. You do not fool yourself with an ego-gratifying "I solved it!" response. In your heart of hearts, you know that you did not solve it. You tried the same thought process that was unsuccessful before, and this time, for no reason you can identify, the answer came. So it is a gift from Something outside your thoughts. Something bigger than your thoughts. Something that can give you the answer when your thought pattern cannot. You become filled with gratitude to the One who has helped you. Receiving the answer is part of your consciousness of God, part of your ongoing relationship with Him. Appreciating God as the source of intellectual success spiritualizes the intellect at its source.

We started with the fact that, so far, science has no demonstrated explanation for finding the answer. But from our perspective, it isn't really necessary. We know that God is behind the so-called "forces of nature." Even if we had an explanation for the source of the answer, we would still express our gratitude to God for creating a natural cause that benefits us in this way. But when we know that we have no such explanation, it is easier to feel it as a gift and recognize God as its source.

The Importance of Stories

We can learn a lot about life from books. But a great deal of life cannot be described in words — it has to be lived. What it feels like to ski, the sound of a sitar, the taste of tortillas, the thrill and fright of the roller coaster, often defy mere verbal description.

There is a middle ground between descriptions and real life: stories. Stories are told in words, but they cause us to live along with the story. We experience the events vicariously, as if we were there. This is crucial, because there are things about life we would like to understand, but we cannot, or definitely do not want to, live through. What it is like to be in a battle, what it is like to die, what it is like to be utterly desperate, or depressed, or terrified…the subjects of literature. The author uses words to describe the feelings that help us understand.

Spirituality is a quality of living. Describing it doesn't do it justice. Although there is no replacement for actual experience, stories help us translate feelings into thoughts.

Let us see what stories can teach us about the spirituality of the intellect.

Here are two true stories.

I. A man's business is failing. He goes to a friend and receives a large loan. Two years later his business has recovered and he comes to repay the loan. The friend refuses the money. "I do not want charity," protests the borrower. His friend says, "I know. I want you to give the money to the next person whose business is failing, and give it with the same condition — that when he recovers, he should do the same for the next person, with the same condition."

One sum of money and one act of kindness will continue to do good and reap benefits forever (unless someone's business never recovers). A person who thinks up such a strategy has taken upon himself to manufacture charity, not just to dispense it. His resources have been used in the most productive way possible. He is not just expressing goodness of character. He is taking responsibility for improving the world.

II. By accident, Peter causes Paul sudden, unexpected, excruciating pain. Paul does not cry out because he does not want to embarrass Peter.

What kind of person is Paul? He is kind, considerate, and sensitive to be sure. But not to cry out from a sudden unexpected pain requires more than that. Paul is psychologically more identified with Peter than he is with his own pain. The pain causes him to think first, "How will Peter feel?" He is fundamentally focused on Peter's welfare. The thought that guides him is "What can I do for him?"

As we read these stories, we think ourselves into their situations and we compare our reactions with theirs. I would never have thought of that way of using my surplus funds. I would never have restrained my cry of pain. I know, from experiencing my own reaction to the story, that I am less spiritual than those people. And I see two ways in which I could seek to grow in order to become more spiritual.

The first story is a direct application of intellect. Even if I were intelligent enough to think of that plan for the money, I wouldn't have because I don't care enough. If I possessed a deep compassion for others, a character trait of God and therefore an expression of spirituality, my intellect would have automatically produced the idea in order to help me enhance my spirituality and my closeness to God.

The second story is even more challenging. Since I am aware that in the same situation I would have cried out, I see that I do not identify with others in that way. That realization is already an application of intellect. Now I can try to understand why my identification with others is so weak, and work on how to strengthen it. (The Mussar movement used personal exercises like volunteering in hospitals and preparing the dead for burial to increase sensitivity to others' pain.) If I do learn to identify better with others, the intellect has helped to make me a more spiritual person.

Biblical Stories

An impoverished widow comes to the prophet Elisha. Her creditors are going to foreclose on her house and take her children as slaves. She has led a life of great spiritual courage — she and her husband hid prophets from the king who wanted to kill them.

Elisha asks her what she has in her house. She replies that all she has is a small container of oil. He tells her to borrow vessels from her neighbors, take her children with her into the house, close the door, and pour the oil from the container into the vessels. She does so, and all the vessels are filled. Elisha then tells her to sell the oil and use the money to pay her creditors and live.

When she poured the oil, did she think to herself, "The container holds six ounces, the barrel holds fifty gallons, the oil will make a thin film on the bottom of the barrel..."? No. She poured the oil with complete trust in God and His prophet, and thought, "The prophet told me to fill the vessels. The six ounces in the container will fill the barrels, the pots, the bowls, and all the other containers." By applying her spirituality to the oil, she actually spiritualized the oil. The oil then received God's blessing and expanded to fill the vessels.

The widow teaches us that the physical exists to serve the spiritual. The physical world is where the spiritual must be expressed. When one does this powerfully enough, the physical world responds in visible ways. This is the meaning of a miracle. The physical leaves its normal pattern in order to visibly serve the spiritual.

The Jews have left Egypt. They reach a body of water, hills to the right and left, and suddenly the Egyptian army is bearing down upon them from behind. Panic! Moses stretches out his arm and the sea splits, allowing the Jews to cross and escape the Egyptians. The physical saves the victim from the oppressor, the innocent from the murderer, the Jews who will receive the Torah from God at Sinai from the Egyptians who administer their cruel empire. The physical serves the spiritual.

Even seemingly ordinary affairs work the same way. King Achashveirosh throws a six-month-long party. At the end he invites his queen to make an appearance. She refuses, so he deposes her. A beauty contest is held to pick a successor. Esther wins the contest and is crowned queen. Mordechai overhears a plot to kill the king. He reports the plot to Esther, she informs the king, and he is saved. The king does not reward Mordechai.

Up to here, do we see any miracle? The king throws a party, an insubordinate queen is replaced, someone has to win the contest, plots against the king are usually unsuccessful (otherwise it would not pay to be king!), and Jews are often not rewarded for their favors.

But now, Haman wants to kill Mordechai and annihilate the Jewish people. He decides to go to the king at night for permission to kill Mordechai. Just that night the king cannot sleep. He orders the history of the kingdom to be read before him. He hears the story of Mordechai saving his life and resolves to reward him. Haman appears and is ordered to honor Mordechai! Esther pleads on behalf of the Jewish people and they are saved.

The king's debt to Mordechai and Esther's position as queen saved the Jewish people. The earlier events were not accidental. They were prepared in advance so that the Jews would be saved. Even seemingly ordinary events are arranged according to God's plans. The physical always serves the spiritual, even when it is not obvious and not a "miracle."

Through the medium of Bible stories, we see the different ways God manifests Himself in different situations. The intellect extrapolates the information, and we can then apply these lessons to the way we view our own lives. God wears a mask. On rare occasions the mask is lowered and we get a glimpse of what lies behind. Then we know that the world is a mask the rest of the time, even when we do not recognize it.

With that in mind, the ordinary, everyday events become special, even precious. The shining sun, the water that quenches our thirst, the solid ground under our feet, every breath — each is a Hand reaching out to us. If we grasp the Hand in every detail of life, then we are spiritual all the time. It is the intellect that gives us the eyes to see His Hand and grasp it.

Puzzles about God

God is good — indeed, He is perfect. And He knows about and can control everything that happens in the world. How then can there be evil? And there is evil! God can prevent it, and, being perfect, it seems He ought to change it. So how can evil exist?

This is not just an abstract philosophical problem. We want to feel that God knows us, and cares about us and for us.

Rampant evil without any explanation makes it hard to feel that way. A person may give up his belief in God altogether in the face of evil. Or he may deaden his sensitivity and close off part of the world from his religious perception. In the first case he suffers spiritual death. In the second case he drastically limits his spirituality by limiting the contexts in which he can relate to God. If the intellect can provide a solution to this problem, his capacity to experience God will be restored.

Here is the solution: Evil can only exist if it is a necessary means to a greater good. For example, when a doctor inoculates a child to immunize him against a disease, the pain is evil. How can we prove this? Simply that next year, when they invent a pill for the same immunization, we do not expect the doctor to continue to use the injection. But now, when the injection is the only way to immunize the child, we tolerate the evil pain for the greater good of the immunization. All the evil in the world is like the pain of the injection.

Many people have experienced near-death, or even clinical death. They see visions, a tunnel or a light, and they hear voices. In addition, when they recover, they have a different appreciation for life. They speak about how precious life is — what a wonderful gift it is. They treasure each day, each opportunity, and each experience. They are more alive after the experience than they were before. Their lives are better — more focused, more sensitive, more profound. They are better off than they were. Now a near-death or clinical death experience is full of pain. Physical pain, fright, despair, and emotional devastation can all be present. Nevertheless, what comes out of the experience is a great good. Most people who have had such experiences are grateful for it.

It does not take such an extreme experience to have a good effect. Often enough it can happen through more ordinary events. Injury, divorce, loss of job, death of a relative or friend, betrayal, loss of money — these events and others can cause a person to question his life. What is really important? What am I doing here? What should my goals be? What are my priorities? Often these questions are not asked because the answers seem so obvious. "I will finish my education, get a job, get married, have children, contribute to my community, have fun and…eventually die. That's it." The "Why" question never arises. But when something disturbs the pattern, then the questions come. And sometimes answers come too.

Sometimes the answers call the whole picture into question.

"My own suffering made me see how much pain there is in the world. So I resolved to do something about it."

"I saw how much I needed support, so I now put much more into my relationships than I did before."

"I realized that I was relying on things that are transient — not reliable. I decided to search for something in life that is really permanent, really absolute."

These people will be grateful for the experiences that lead them to their new insights and orientation to life.

The experiences were painful, and yet they led to a better life. Now some of the pain we experience in this world is God's way of trying to wake us up. "You are lost in the sandbox, you are playing with the electric trains. That is not what life is about! Look again!" In this way God uses evil to bring about good.

Free Will

Free will is what makes man capable of spirituality altogether. Why do we not describe animals as kind or cruel, just or unjust, fair or unfair, generous or miserly? And why do we not describe machines in these ways? The answer is that they don't make free choices. They are completely determined by their internal "programming" to do what they do. If people were like that, they would not be responsible for their actions. It is only because we make free choices that we are responsible, and then those choices can be kind or cruel, just or unjust, etc.

So our ability to perfect ourselves depends upon free will. Now what does free will itself depend on? There has to be a reasonable psychological balance between the choice of good and the choice of evil. Our motivation has to be divided so that free will can decide between them. If we are not attracted in both directions, free will cannot make a choice.

The balance is achieved by giving the person two parts, the soul and the body. One is naturally attracted to good, and the other to evil. The person is thus pulled in both directions, and the free will can make the choice.

World Balance

But this is not enough — soul and body. The world has to be balanced between good and evil also, otherwise we will not be psychologically free to choose.

For example, suppose every time you do something good, there is an immediate, tangible reward. And every time you do something bad, there is an immediate, tangible punishment. Then when the choice comes, you know the consequences. The payoff is clearly all on one side. These are not balanced choices.

To have balanced choices, the good must often lead to loss and suffering, while the bad must lead to profit and pleasure often enough that the body is really drawn to the bad, and the person is really divided within himself.

This is one reason why there is evil in the world. Why must

good people suffer and bad people prosper much of the time? Because if it were not so, good people would not be good! They would simply be choosing their own benefit and avoiding their own loss. Being good means choosing the good, and in order to choose the good — really choose it — you have to be prepared to suffer for it. Only then is the choice balanced, so that the good is chosen for its own sake. Only then can the choice of good express goodness rather than self-interest.

The Need for Evil

Why should the body be regarded as naturally evil? Can anything created by God really be evil?

As we explained before, evil can exist only when it is a means to a greater good. So the body is a vehicle for good, even if it is naturally evil.

What do we mean by "evil?" Here there is a problem. We call two different kinds of things evil: suffering and crime. When there is suffering, we want to know how God can allow it in His world. When innocent people suffer (or even partly guilty people suffer far more than their bad actions deserve) it seems unfair, wrong — evil.

Crime is also evil, even if no one suffers. Stealing ten dollars from a millionaire is wrong — evil — even if he will never notice the theft.

Now why should we use the same word for two such different types of things? The answer is that the root of all evil is one thing: being out of touch with God. If God is hidden or distant, if a person is "cut off" from God, that is evil.

Suffering and crime hide God's presence. That is why they are both called evil. God's purpose for the creation is a joyous relationship with Him. Pain is not the purpose. It is only a means. Thus when we see pain and suffering we do not perceive God's presence. He is hidden in the pain.

Free will enables man to express God's presence. When he does God's will, then we see God in the person's actions. When a person commits a crime, when he violates God's will, then his action hides God's presence. We do not see God in him. We only see something opposing God's will.

So suffering and crime both hide God's presence. That is why they are evil. Now according to this definition of evil, God Himself does evil.

How could it be that God does evil?

Let's take it apart. The root of evil is being separated from God, His being hidden. The whole creation hides His presence. The appearance of nature makes the world look as if it has no direction, no purpose. It was made that way intentionally. God hid Himself, and that is evil.

But, this evil has a purpose. We said before that if He had not hidden himself, then we would not have free will. Without free will we have no good at all. So this is like every case of evil: a means to a greater good. But that does not take away the fact that it is evil, evil that God Himself does.

So now we understand why there is evil in the world. Yes, God created the world in order to do good, to benefit His creatures. He created the world to express His love of His creatures. But in order to do that, He gave us free will, and that has a cost. The cost is that God hides His presence, and that means that we temporarily live with evil. He also uses suffering — evil — to help us focus our lives, to become more alive.

This changes the way we experience the pain and human failure that touch our lives. The hurt is real and should not be denied. But together with the hurt, we should remember the purpose. It is like the doctor. However much he apologizes, the surgery still hurts. But when it is over we thank him, because we know it was for our good. In the same way, we can feel grateful that God cares enough for us to bring us to the best possible circumstances, even though we might be in pain at the same time.

Once the intellect understands the purpose of evil, we can experience God, and even love Him, in the midst of the evil. It will no longer be a barrier to living in a conscious love relationship with God, and a fully spiritual life.

Commandments

Laws, obligations, responsibilities, reward, punishment — sounds dismal! A healthy diet, exercises that improve your memory, meditation to make you more sensitive and caring, insight that improves deep personal relationships — sounds wonderful! Now suppose they are the same. Think of laws that will make you healthier, more sensitive and caring, give you better relationships. You are on the way to understanding the commandments.

Jewish laws are paths of contact with God. The contact is the reward. Violating a law reduces contact, and that itself is the punishment.

The law uses the intellect in three ways: the intellect understands what the laws say, the intellect understands the reasons for the laws, and the intellect understands the world to which the law applies.

The intellect understands what the laws say. A lawyer has to use his brains. He learns a great amount of information. He distinguishes categories. He learns arguments. He interprets texts. He recognizes contradictions and objections. This applies to the study of Jewish law as well. Information is mastered, categories recognized, arguments learned, and objections and contradictions are resolved.

But it is much more than that. When we study Jewish law, we are learning the will of God. We are filling our minds with the "thoughts" of God, attuning our minds to Him. This study brings the mind into relationship with God and is therefore inherently spiritual. We see and experience God through the intellect when we study Torah.

The intellect understands the reasons for the laws. Every law has reasons. Every law helps perfect the person who performs it. It constructs some part of our relationship with God. When we learn some of these reasons, the performance of a law becomes much more spiritual.

Why is it more spiritual? Well, how do we feel when we perform a law? There is a feeling of obedience — this is what God wills and I accept it — as well as comfort in the knowledge that each specific law adds a dimension of connection with God that no other law can provide. (That is why this particular law exists.)

The law can add this dimension of relationship with God even if we are not aware of it. But imagine we are aware. Then it is possible to feel the precious impact of the law, to feel the love of the One who gave the law for the sake of my perfection, and I feel my love for Him in return. So when I perform the law, I am bathed in love. The relationship is much deeper, more profound, and more intense. So the actual performance of the law is more spiritual.

The intellect understands the world to which the law applies. We fast on Yom Kippur, but not if fasting will endanger life. How do we know if fasting will be dangerous? From medicine. There is a law to be fruitful and multiply. This means that problems of infertility must be overcome, again, by medicine. A sukkah must have an area of at least forty-nine square handbreadths. Suppose it is round — how big must the diameter be? The answer comes from mathematics. Is a fluorescent lightbulb fire for the laws of the Sabbath? The answer will come from physics. To apply the law to the world we must understand many aspects of the world. It is the intellect that supplies the understanding.

Understanding the world in order to apply the law spiritualizes the intellect. We look at the world as the creation of God. Its purpose is to be a bridge to Him. We study it as a creation, as a trigger for the law that will express our relationship with God.

There is more. Woe to he who has not eyes to see the beauty of the world! And double woe to he who has the eyes, but has not the mind to understand what he sees. We see the intricacy of the flower, the roots, stalk and petals, the pistil and stamen, the cells absorbing nutrition and dividing to provide growth, the tropisms guiding the roots to the water and the petals to the sun. And we understand that this is the product of the will of God. And then, because we understand, we are filled with awe of God.

Beyond the intellectual connection, the simple beauty of the flower inspires us. When we understand that God created that beauty, and gave us the ability to perceive and appreciate it, we are filled with gratitude for Him. We feel the love of God for us in the beauty of the world, and we respond in love.

In all these ways, the intellect is part of the spirit.

A Spiritual Mind

Why must the intellect be part of our spirituality? What is wrong with mindless feeling, floating through life on clouds of contented dreams?

Let's go back to the beginning. Spirituality is living in a conscious love relationship with God. Now love wants to include the whole person. Imagine that there is something about you that you cannot share with your beloved. It is too embarrassing to reveal. Isn't there something missing in your relationship with your beloved? Would you not be relieved if you found a way to finally share that part of yourself?

You have a mind. If spirituality does not use it, then part of you is left out. If spirituality is loving God, then leaving out part of yourself is not tolerable. Love wants a total relationship, a connection of all of you with the beloved. That is why the mind must be part of spirituality.

Now look at it from the other side. God created the mind. Spirituality is the whole purpose of the creation and everything in it. So the intellect must be part of spirituality, otherwise it would not have been created.

We said at the beginning that "spirituality" is different in different cultures. In this respect, the Jewish way differs sharply. Many would have you turn your back on your intellect. For them, the mind is the enemy. Contemplation is designed to short-circuit the mind. Only with the mind turned off can you reach beyond this illusion of a world to the "reality" beyond, they say.

They are not reaching God. They are missing the point. It is they who are out of touch. They do not appreciate that everything comes from a single Source that created each thing as a bridge to reach God. This includes the intellect.

We might ask: If contemplation is the best path for man, if we should remove ourselves from the world, if the ideal is the focus on the inner reality at the core without distractions from the outside, then why isn't God doing that? Why is there a world at all? God can do as He pleases. God is perfect, so He will do the best, the ideal. If the ideal for us is contemplation, why doesn't God just contemplate Himself?

The ideal for man is to become as much like God as he can. If God is creative, if God makes a world in order to give good to His creatures, then it makes sense for man to be creative and giving. If God is creative and good, and man is told to just contemplate, then he is being told to become the opposite of God!

Use your mind. Use it to connect. Focus your conscious attention on God; use your intellect to maximize your connections with God through all of your resources. Integrate the intellect with your spirituality, and you can bring yourself to be whole in spirit as you live together with God.

Mimi L. Deutsch Dickman

EMOTIONAL
INTEGRATION

Mimi L. Deutsch Dickman, BA, MEd, MS Psych, holds a BA from Hebrew University in philosophy and French literature, a Master's Degree in philosophy and psychology of education from Boston University, and a Master of Science Degree in clinical psychology from the City University of New York. Mrs. Dickman spent ten years of her early life in instruction in Jewish education in Israel and New York, and many more years teaching and lecturing on Jewish education. Later, she served as staff psychologist in a special child and family unit at the Peninsula Counseling Center in Woodmere, New York. Today, Mrs. Dickman continues to lecture on topics of Jewish interest and psychology, while managing a private practice in creating wellness through work in creative imagery and treatment of trauma in Jerusalem.

INTRODUCTION

The soul is the spiritual part of the human being that continues to exist after the body dies. In Judaism, the soul is regarded as a "piece of the infinite," which during life gathers experiences, emotions, and the thoughts that remain in its memory after death.

Judaism views basic needs as manifestations of the soul. It does not ignore or repress the human desires for meaning, intimacy, and comfort, but promotes a lifestyle in which these are balanced in a soulful context. This is one reason the Torah, God's blueprint for living, is so focused on practical application. It is much more than a social and legal code; it is nothing less than a formula for the soul to harness the powers of the body to fulfill its mission on earth. Life is lived to the fullest when the body and soul are in harmony.

The Torah teaches great ideals, good for emotional well-being. For example, that all human beings are created in the image of God; that all are responsible for their deeds; that human beings must have compassion for each other and not try to convert or coerce the other; and that generosity is superior to greed.

Humans are born pure: "Very good" is how the Bible describes the creation of humankind (Genesis 1:31). The soul was, is, and always will be a Divine property. Though at times we may obscure this purity, we all, with rare exception, eventually return to that state. The harmony between body and soul during life determines the soul's experiences after life. If a body-soul system is balanced and fulfilled in life, ultimately the soul will enter into a state of en-

joyment of the Divine where the soul is reconnected with its source, devoid of ego, hurt, and resentment. The Talmud says that a person's ultimate future is determined by his own choices. The body and soul are in a relationship and a person chooses which one will guide the decisions of life.

Freud said the basis of all neurosis is not relating to reality. There is no greater reality than the fact that God is the King of the world, and reality should be dealt with on those terms. Since He created us, He certainly knows what we need and what is best for us — to serve Him with joy. Only being cognizant of this will allow us to achieve the harmony which is the essence of our own well-being.

Mimi L. Deutsch Dickman

THE JOURNEY BACK TO EDEN

t first glance, the topics of emotional health and Judaism seem incompatible. Judaism is a religion with a set of beliefs, laws, and practices. What possible connection could there be between a body of religious law and a human being's psychological well-being?

To answer this question we must inquire about what constitutes psychological well-being. Does it mean feeling happy all the time? Does it mean living without any symptoms of anxiety, worry, or depression? Does it mean having the ability to function well in a complex, modern world? Jewish history and law emphasize the belief that "living properly" — bringing into fulfillment the purpose for which man was created — has the potential to create a life which is ever creative, unfolding, and dynamic. As it is written, "And thou shalt keep My statutes and laws, that man should observe them and live with them" (Leviticus 18:5), indicating that the precepts of the Torah are meant to enhance life.

Nature in the Garden of Eden — Who Is Man Supposed to Be?

How can we reach an understanding of what man was meant to be, if not through the study of the original scene in which man was introduced into the world, in the Garden of Eden? The Book of Genesis unfolds before us the most idyllic and perfectly balanced state of being, a view of nature wherein chaos has been replaced by matter, with a shape, form, and a perfecting sorting of all species and sorts within the natural world. God separates between the light and the darkness, the day and the night, the upper and lower waters, species of plant and fruit, and types on the earth, the sea, and the sky.

To understand man's nature and purpose we open to the first chapter of Genesis, where God seeks counsel with the angels. "Let us make man in Our image, after Our likeness" (Genesis 1:26), declares God, a statement which creates the paradigm for man's attitude towards others in the world. Man, who carries in him the spirit of God, is here to mirror God's behavior and so to develop his greatest potential. Just as God is humble, modest, and, though all-knowing, turns to the angels to include them in His great endeavor, so must man embody these traits to fulfill his most basic mission on earth. Basic to man's role is the recognition that he is, by himself, insufficient. The prophet Micah later reaffirms the importance of humility when he says, "[God] has told you, man, what is good and what God asks of you, but to do justice, and to love compassion, and to walk humbly with your God" (6:8).

God creates man, and then woman of man, and sets into motion a world of perfect order. All of nature and the animal kingdom are to live in harmony under man's rule, between sea and sky. God gives man one commandment, which he has the power to obey or disobey. This is the only variable, and all of world history pivots around it. Through the Tree of Knowledge, man must make the choice to live eternally or quest for knowledge.

Man, in true form, thinking to fulfill his Godlike potential, "wants" desperately to know. The snake then introduces the all-time killer of faith — doubt. He convinces Eve that the injunction against eating from the Tree of Knowledge is God's ploy to keep man forever subservient; that perhaps man could supersede God, if he could gain all knowledge by eating from the tree. It is at this point that the first conflict arises. Man has the opportunity to choose between faith (in God) over doubt (the snake). Reason and trust give way to fear, as well as temptation and curiosity, and man falters, casting the entire world into exile.

Though at that moment mankind loses its opportunity for eternal life, man is compensated by retaining the most sacred human quality, the gift of choice, which holds the potential for escorting man back to the garden of harmony and wholeness. Wholeness is now merely a memory of the perfect relationship with the Creator. The natural integration of body and soul, now disintegrated, could only be regained through conscious and positive choice. Man's unity now depends on his doing, his only guide the faint "smell of the field [of Eden]" (*Midrash Rabbah* on Genesis 22:55), planted deeply in his unconscious memory.

One of the effects of this sudden and unforeseen fall is that man is left without a well-developed identity in his relationship with God, but with a great desire to return to his original wholeness. He must begin to ask the questions: What is my role here? Who am I supposed to be? What does it mean to be a child of God? How can man be mind, spirit, and body? First

Abraham and later the Torah enters at this point to offer man the gift of his true and rightful identity. The Torah offers guidelines and positive commandments in every realm of life, which help realign man with his original purpose and function in the world, in an attempt to turn him back in the direction of Eden. The Torah, in the Five Books of Moses, explains clearly that in order for man to live well, according to the original design, he must know his place in the world matrix. He must know where he stands in relation to the rest of creation and God. This knowledge, lost with the fall, is regained only later through the courageous efforts of Abraham.

The Mistakes of History

Twenty generations elapsed between Adam and Abraham, where the world existed almost completely without man's active relationship with God. After the murders of Abel and later Cain, mankind removed itself from God, profanity and paganism were rampant, and the schism between man's original bliss and the subsequent fall widened. This was further evidenced by the generation of the flood, where boundary after boundary was invaded through theft, robbery, and distortion of all the natural laws of animal and human behavior. The Midrash tells us that the earth itself was corrupted by mankind, as all of creation follows man's model. Next came the Tower of Babel, in which mankind tried to unite, but ended up fighting with God.

As a result of his loneliness and fear in a seemingly godless world, man tried to become his own god, leaving himself more lonely and in despair, with more cause to wage war in order to establish a haven of security through his superiority over others. These beliefs offered little substitute for a real identity of substance for man.

The Cataclysmic Discovery of Abraham

Abraham is crowned the "Father of a multitude of nations" (Genesis 15:4) because he restores to the world its long-lost identity. He brings God back into the universe as its Creator, realigns man with Him as a partner in creation, rather than a rival, and brings congeniality and peacefulness into the world, rather than war. How does Abraham achieve this?

Abraham recognizes the truth of God's existence. Since he recognizes that he, too, is sustained by Him, he must affirm this truth even as far as risking his life in Nimrod's burning furnace. Having heard of the justice meted out through the flood and the punishment of the Tower of Babel, Abraham recognizes with manifest clarity the presence of a Divine Creator. He understands that this is the same Master of the Universe who has vested within him his own spirit of life. Without the acknowledgment of this truth, his very own life would be worthless. Receiving blessing from a benevolent God is contingent upon crowning him as Master. Children receive the benefits of love and security from their parents, because they recognize them as their parents and engage in such relationship with them. It then becomes reciprocal. That is what Adam and Eve had in Eden, which Abraham now reestablishes.

By engaging in relationship and creating a covenant with God, Abraham returns a parent to the world permanently, and reestablishes man's and the world's identity vis-à-vis God. In this relationship man finds himself. God is a parent, a friend, a support, an example to emulate, and a container for all that man can become. The world can again establish an identity. As God saves Abraham from the burning furnace, he becomes a Benevolent Creator, dependable and loving, sustaining and caring.

Man, whose spirit is rooted in the singular spirit of God, lives a physical life but is able to invest this spirit in anything he does. He has the potential to work with God as a partner, as he yearns to reunite with Him in wholeness. He can become godly, but he cannot be God. The homocentric universe of self-centered man turns into a God-centered universe with man as His conduit, here on earth to deliver God's Divine message through his actions.

Abraham did for the world what good parents do for their children. Parents give their children a context and a structure. They teach their children who they are, what family they belong to, what the rules are in the family, and how all these things make them who they are. Then, the children can get down to the task of living. They feel safe and secure, and they can explore and develop their world.

Abraham recognizes that God sustains the world the way parents feed and nurture their children, a process without which we would all perish. Abraham helps man connect through the soul to understand that man's mission on earth is to kindle our spirits so as to bring the Divine into our daily lives. This why Abraham and Sarah are said to have "made souls," for they brought mankind to the knowledge of God. The Talmud actually praises Abraham for building the world through love, as a mason constructs a house with stone. When King David declares, "The world is created through lovingkindness" (Psalms 89:3), the Sages tell us that he is speaking of Abraham, who actually achieved this.

Children generally fear and respect their parents. This is what gives validity to the parent-child relationship and helps the child model himself after his parents. There is an identification process that develops as a result of this dependency. Later in his development the child differentiates and can love his parents, not only because they afford him safety and protection, but because they have developed an intimate bond with him. In order for mankind to receive the benefits of a Creator, they must identify with Him, by doing as He does, by looking toward Him, by yearning for His closeness, by recognizing that He brings to us something invaluable, the essence of our very existence. Abraham discovers that such a relationship is possible with God. Like children, for this we are grateful. We are also humbled by recognizing the all-powerful goodness which we need and receive with benevolence.

If we return for a moment to the concept of humility at this point, we can understand why "humility" is necessarily introduced at the inception of man. In man's humility, he recognizes himself as living in God's world; all that he receives, then, becomes a blessing. It helps us find our place in the world's mosaic — and knowing one's place is the first step towards achieving wholeness.

The Blessings of Humility

How does humility actually help us in our journey back to Eden? We all know that it is a pleasure to be in the company of a person who is truly humble. But what makes it so? In essence, it is our legacy from Abraham, whose journey and gift of trust begins with his introspective descent into self, understanding his human limits, turning to God for help, and receiving it with faith. Humility leaves space for "the other person" (and, of course, for God) and gives value to the existence and contribution of every human being. When we act with humility we can express appreciation for another person and also indicate that we respect what he can give to us, or what we are able to receive from him. In our competitive world, so much emphasis is put on personal performance and achievement. We emphasize what we can give or contribute to the world, but rarely do we value the potential contribution of the person sitting next to us. We want to be heard, but how often do we listen? Actually, humility helps to bring us into relationship with our fellowman. It teaches us that we need him. Furthermore, in humility there is a tacit understanding that his contribution to the world can be as important as our own.

If we return to Abraham, we see that Abraham's enlightenment actually clarified this point greatly. Once he accepted God as the Provider, Ruler, Master, and Parent of the universe, he recognized his dependency upon Him along with his own limitation. The awareness of his limitation brings Abraham to a point of deep humility. Abraham's willingness to circumcise himself at God's command shows that he is putting himself in God's hands, and his future will now be subject to God's determinations and not his own. The relationship with God brings man to a level of spirit and importance, but that level will always be limited by virtue of the fact that it is in relation to God. Man can be great, but he will forever remain man.

As Abraham hones his relationship with God by enduring test after test, this message of blessing through faith becomes clearer. As the child and partner of God, we receive security, sustenance, and also partnership in the grand production of the world. Man can leave his fear and egocentricity and begin to have faith that there is a benevolent force guiding the world. His security will bring him to trust, and away from fear, which will leave him free to do the work of "conquering the world." The same paradigm expresses itself in human development, where toddlers in the stage of exploration are willing to leave the dependent phase of life and opt for the more interesting venue of "discovery." However, they are able to successfully undertake and achieve success in this exploratory phase only if they feel secure. The secure presence of an available parent, who is "there" so the child may come and go with sufficient ease, is all that is necessary to accompany a child out of dependency and into exploration.

Abraham shows the world that what God actually wants is to be that capacitating parent, one who can facilitate the growth of his children. He can remain available and "in contact" with us, the key to good exploration, and stay encouraging of our earthly endeavors. Abraham teaches the world that we are not alone and that we can "trust" God. Our limitation leads to humility and finally into a relationship of trust with God. It is by connecting to God, then, that we become empowered, rendering us more able to weather the vicissitudes of life and build a great world. This connection to God and his tenets brings back the light that was lost in Eden, and allows man to come still closer to his original purpose in creation. Man no longer feels the need to rival God, because he can trust, and in trust he can humbly receive the blessing that he needs. This is the beginning of love.

Abraham essentially reverses the process that originated in the fall from Eden, where fear and doubt broke the relationship with God. Bonds are made through trust, and bonds are healed through trust. Now, through trusting, Abraham heals the wound of civilization and returns the world to its rightful place in creation.

Humility and Mental Health

As we described above, humility, which is real, helps a person know where he belongs. Most emotional difficulties could be briefly summed up as imbalances of the ego. Good ego function realizes its limitations; it is neither grandiose nor is it self-destructive, neither arrogant nor self-abnegating. It is the clarity and balance in self-perception that creates emotional health. Good psychology also teaches us that we must accept our human limitations as they are, while simultaneously rejoicing over the potentialities of what we can be. This allows us to grow.

Seeing clearly who we are will help us understand that we are all dependent, and we are all interdependent. The lesson that Abraham taught us is that we have a crucial role to play in the world, but only if we can accept who we are. For we need to know that along with the gifts we receive from heaven, we need also from our fellowman. Each human being is significant for the potential he has to bring into this world, but no man is sufficient in and of himself.

Ultimately, the lesson of humility brings us to love, because when we recognize our limitations and needs, we can truly appreciate how much others have to offer us, and we can see them as friends, rather than competitors. If we see only limitations in ourselves, then we cannot contribute to the world. This is the legacy of Avraham. He turns doubt and fear to love, by investing in faith. By trusting God, he realizes that the spirit of the Benevolent Creator exists in all of mankind. This brings him to love mankind as representations of the Creator on earth.

We might ask: What if man does not reflect his Creator properly, can we still love him? The answer would be "surely," for man carries with him that potential for goodness always. It is a question of helping him express his godliness. This is why Abraham is known as the father of lovingkindness, because he makes that link between the benevolence of God and that characteristic in human beings. He then teaches how it is possible to love mankind. Ultimately, love of oneself leads to love of mankind, both of which originate in love and acceptance of the Creator of the Universe, as the Source of all good.

Abraham, then, gets the world back on the path of clear

thinking and putting the pieces of the world mosaic back into order. By clarifying man's purpose on earth, he helps people learn that they need each other to carry out their own final purpose. The world can't be built by one person; it needs the cooperative efforts of all people, which means that trust is needed for human relationship as well. Having taught the world this lesson, the possibility of bringing light into the world reappears, and with it the possibility of spreading that light from soul to soul.

Wholeness in Judaism

If wholeness is what is needed to return to our original state, then Abraham's joining with God in partnership was the first step in returning man to his original place. Changing doubt and fear to trust and love corrected the original mistake, and put man in a place where he could receive from God and also enjoy the blessings of creating loving relations with his fellowman. This is exactly what the mitzvot, the commandments, do, for they create a concrete path through which man can return to his original state of rhythm with the world — plant, animal, and man. The entire realm of commandments that deal with behavior toward our fellowman instructs us on proper interpersonal behavior. The commandments regarding our relationship with God help us connect with our Creator. These laws deal with all aspects of life, including plants and animals, and help us restore the supremacy we had in the idyllic state of Eden, where man was truly able to be in harmony with his world. Living within that state of perfect balance renews our perception of reality as it was meant to be, in harmony with all of nature, and permits us to see "goodness."

A chassidic tale is told of the afterlife. A sage visited a group of souls in the World to Come. He entered one room, where there was an elegant feast with sumptuous foods laid out on tables of gold and silver. There were magnificent fruits and dishes of varied delight. Many people were seated at this banquet, but they all had three-foot-long knives and forks strapped to their arms, so they were forced to sit at the tables and simply gaze at the food, without partaking of any of it. This was Hell. He walked into the next room, where he saw a similar feast — tables bedecked with delicious pots of meats and fish, breathtaking fruits, and a multitude of desserts. In this room, too, the people had three-foot-long knives and forks strapped to their arms, but here each individual was feeding the person sitting across the table from him. This was Heaven.

If man could return in conscious faith to take the place he was meant to take in earthly life, vis-à-vis God and his fellowman, through making the positive choice to act in accordance with his true nature, the possibility of the return to Eden and the redemption of mankind could be realized. The acceptance of Torah life makes this possible.

Yaakov Levinson

PHYSICAL
INTEGRATION

Yaakov Levinson *is an internationally known nutrition consultant, author, and researcher. He is the author of the groundbreaking work,* The Jewish Guide to Natural Nutrition. *As well, he has presented original research both at the 12th (Philippines, 1996) and 13th (Scotland, 2000) International Congresses of Dietetics. He holds a Bachelor of Arts degree (BA) in biology from Hamilton College, Clinton, New York, and earned a master's degree (MS) in clinical nutrition from Case Western Reserve University in Cleveland, Ohio (1976).*

Levinson's professional experience began at Memorial Hospital in Albany, New York, where he published a hospital manual on clinical nutrition. He then moved to Jerusalem, where he specializes in weight management, as well as surgical and geriatric nutrition.

INTRODUCTION

When we think about Torah scholars and Orthodox Jews, we might conjure up a picture of rabbis hunched over large volumes day and night, with no thought to their physical being.

This image couldn't be further from the truth! Because Judaism is a discipline which encompasses all aspects of our lives, taking care of our bodies is a top priority. The Torah views the body as a tool and as a vehicle for the soul. If the body is weak or ill, the soul's power is diminished, and along with it, a person's ability to perfect himself in this world is also lessened. The Maggid of Mezritch said it a different way: one who creates a small defect in the body creates a small defect in the soul.

A sage of the Talmud is recorded as saying that he had to feed his body because it depended on him to look after it. God gave us our bodies for safekeeping, and we have to look after them just the same as anything else that is left in our care that doesn't belong to us. The Torah outlines specific rules pertaining to physical health, including proper diet and hygiene, and we are also required to avoid any unnecessary risks and detrimental behaviors like smoking, overeating, and substance abuse. One who fulfills this ideal will use the world to best maintain his health and preserve his life.

The Rambam's ideal is a person who keeps himself healthy primarily by proper living and only resorting to medicine when in need of a cure. This person will act responsibly according to natural laws, including taking medicine when need be to sustain and preserve his life, but whose goal for doing so is to promote his service of God.

Yaakov Levinson

NUTRITION: AN ELEVATED MEAL

Our very existence in this world revolves around physical and mundane pursuits. Yet we are told that our soul's task on this earth has nothing to do with our physical existence: "What does Hashem demand of you? Only to fear God" (Deuteronomy 10:12).

The act of eating, for example, though necessary for survival, is so utterly earthly that it has the potential to drag us down to very low spiritual levels. Our challenge is to purify the act of eating, to turn the food we eat into a Heavenly sustenance of the spirit.

The Torah says, "And you shall eat and be satisfied and bless God" (Deuteronomy 8:10). The sages of the Talmud explain that if one's desire in eating is only to be satisfied and not to indulge in gluttony, then one is considered to be "blessing God." When we elevate our food further with the blessings and commandments associated with eating, our eating becomes a spiritual act like the performance of any other commandment. Thus even the food we eat can become a substance that raises us spiritually. In fact, all of our physical acts can bring us closer to God depending on how we perform them.

But why is our grace after meals described as "blessing God"? Everyone accepts that it is important to thank God for sustaining us. But for us to bless God seems paradoxical. What can we give God that He doesn't already have?

We have to consider why the Talmudic sages determined that the blessing after meals is to be said only on meals that include bread. What is so special about bread that it should be distinguished from all other foods?

One explanation concerns the level of partnership with God inherent in the different types of agriculture. In growing fruit, the human end of the partnership is limited. Once the tree is grown, God provides the fertile soil and rain according to His will. The finished product is edible as is. But making bread is a much more interactive process, not only involving sowing, plowing, reaping, and threshing every year, and but also sifting, kneading, and baking every time one wants to eat. Thus, producing bread is a much more human (and labor-intensive) endeavor. God provides the seed, the earth, the sun, and the rain, but without the talents and labor of human beings the seed would never be transformed into bread. This is human partnership with God at its maximum.

The greater the degree of human involvement, the greater the need to recognize Divine participation. God chose to create an incomplete and imperfect world so that we could become His partners in perfecting the world, and by doing so, perfect ourselves. By purposefully cooperating with God's design and raising our spirituality as a result of it, we indeed bless God.

The Baal Shem Tov said, "By the manner in which you eat you serve God." If not performed with holiness, the act of eating is simply an instinctive act necessary to preserve life in our bodies or a means of satisfying our greed. But performed in holiness, the act of eating becomes very spiritual.

The Proverbs say that "A righteous person eats to satisfy his soul."

Children with poor table manners are told by their parents "You are eating like an animal!" Yet animals eat only for their bodily needs. They do not overeat or indulge in eating pleasures like humans do.

People who sincerely believe they are on earth only to serve God eat to sustain their life and to have energy to fulfill their earthly assignment. They may enjoy eating, but do not indulge themselves or seek ways to enhance their food. And, because they consume only food necessary for optimal bodily function, they are unlikely to become obese.

Maimonides, a twelfth-century physician, stated that the majority of human ills come from unhealthy eating practices. This has been substantiated by modern medical science.

Humbling is the thought that if humans did eat like animals, they would live longer and healthier!

A Wholly Diet

Like the body itself, the food we eat is actually a combination of both physical and spiritual entities. The body is nourished by the nutrients in the food, and the soul is nourished by the sparks of holiness which enliven anything physical, including food. Therefore, the body and the soul are united in the act of eating.

Just like all of creation is made up of a mixture of good and evil, in every food there is also a combination of good and evil.

Food consists of useful parts like nutrients, and disposable aspects like waste or indigestible matter. Likewise, spiritually, food contains sparks of holiness, which are good components, and husks or *klippot*, which are the gross, bad components that encompass the sparks.

In the Beginning...

God put man in the Garden of Eden and told him he could eat from every tree there except the Tree of Knowledge of Good and Evil. Soon after God created the first woman, Chava, they ate from the tree. If they would have waited until Shabbos, a few hours later, they could have eaten the fruit with God's blessings. But with that one bite, they introduced desire for all material, bodily pleasures and for all sins. Whereas before, good and evil were separate, they now became mixed together. Pure became mixed with the impure, and it was very hard to separate it out.

But there is hope...

Spiritual Origins: The Sparks

Before descending into the body, the soul is nourished as the angels are, directly from God. Once the soul comes into the world, the body separates it from this spiritual and direct form of sustenance. In this world, the soul is nourished by physical food, which is the physical counterpart to the Divine food it once ate. So when one eats, he can still benefit a little from the radiance of the *Shechinah*.

Eating is one of our most common activities. It is part of God's plan that we are so involved in eating. There is an important spiritual purpose to it. If we really can separate good from evil by eating correctly, then this purification and separation can affect all levels of reality, and be a rectification for that original mixing that took place in the Garden of Eden.

When a person recites blessings on the food or uses the strength from food to perform a commandment, he can send the sparks of holiness in the food back to Heaven from where they had originally fallen! The sparks of holiness are thereby returned to their source.

As the rain falls from above and helps the earth send forth vegetation, as animals feed on plants and other animals, and as man raises mineral, vegetable, and animal matter up to its source by serving God, then all the sparks of holiness are raised and returned to their source in Heaven, and the way will be paved for our final redemption!

You Are What You Eat

Overeating is like poison to anyone's body. Many illnesses which afflict a man are caused by harmful foods or by his filling his belly and overeating, even of healthful foods.

Whoever guards his mouth and his tongue guards his soul from distress. Guarding the mouth refers to eating harmful food or eating too much, and guarding the tongue refers to speaking about things other than his needs.

Therefore, we must not eat whatever is palatable just like the dog and the donkey, but only the things that are helpful to and good for the health of the body. There are some saintly people who, before partaking of food or drink, say, "I am ready to eat and drink in order that I may gain health and strength to worship the Creator, blessed be His name."

Some Practical Advice

Good nutrition can be ensured by eating a varied diet of fresh wholesome foods. These foods should be, as much as possible, unrefined and high in complex carbohydrates and fiber, adequate but not excessive in protein, and low in fat, cholesterol, and salt.

Changes in eating, however, cannot and should not be made overnight. Gradually improving your diet is the best way to ensure good health and long-term change. Begin by reducing high-fat foods, especially fatty meats, fried foods, eggs, and milk products high in fat. Then take one step at a time, progressing to a diet based on grains and legumes, vegetables and fruits, low-fat milk products, and, if you wish, low-fat fish and poultry.

Food as an Atonement

As we keep all of the physical and spiritual aspects of food in mind, we can remember that the table on which we eat is taking the place of the altar in the Beis HaMikdash, the Holy Temple in Jerusalem. As long as the Temple stood, the sacrificial altar atoned for Israel. Now a man's table atones for him. During the times of our Temple, a chief effect of sacrificing was the elevation and purification of the sparks of holiness contained in the sacrifices. Now that we no longer have the Temple service, our prayers and eating serve this function.

Our eating for this elevated purpose, for the sake of Heaven, can bring us to holiness and to closeness with God.

Dr. Moshe Kaplan

HEAVEN CAN WAIT

In 1978, Dr. Lester Breslow and associates at the UCLA School of Medicine identified seven basic, simple habits which could be relied on to increase life expectancy:

1. Eat three regular meals daily and no between-meal snacks.

2. Eat breakfast.

3. Keep body weight within the normal range.

4. Get regular exercise.

5. Get seven to eight hours of sleep each night.

6. Do not smoke.

7. Limit alcohol intake to two drinks daily or less.

Maimonides, the Rambam, has these recommendations for healthy living:

1. Only eat when hungry; only drink when thirsty (in a temperate climate).

2. Go to the bathroom promptly when the need is felt.

3. Don't eat to the point of feeling stuffed — leave the stomach a bit empty.

4. Don't drink while eating.

5. Don't eat until the body has warmed up through exercise.

6. Sit comfortably in your place while eating.

7. Sleep eight hours a day.

8. Don't sleep immediately after eating.

9. Eat healthy foods, especially ripe, high-fiber fruits and vegetables in season.

10. Exercise daily.

Hundreds of research studies document the link between faith and health. Among the positive effects of piety:

Longer life. A nationwide study of 21,000 people, conducted between 1987 and 1995, found a seven-year difference in life expectancy between those who never attend religious services and those who attend more than once a week.

Overall Well-Being. In research co-conducted by epidemiologist Jeff Levin, author of *God, Faith, and Health*, older adults who considered themselves religious had fewer health problems and functioned better than the nonreligious.

Better Recovery. Patients comforted by their faith had three times the chance of being alive six months after open-heart surgery than patients who found no comfort in religion, a 1995 Dartmouth Medical School study found.

Lower Blood Pressure. In a 1989 study of 400 Caucasian men in Evans County, Georgia, Duke researchers found a significant protective effect against high blood pressure among those who considered religion very important and attended church regularly.

Good Mental Health. Attendance at a house of worship is related to lower rates of depression and anxiety, reported a 1999 Duke University study of nearly 4000 older adults.

In addition, a Duke University study of 150 patients suffering from acute heart disease showed that patients prayed for did significantly better than those who were not prayed for, even when the patient was completely unaware of the prayers on his behalf.

And if that is not enough, developing your spiritual side may help keep you out of the hospital. In a study of older adults, the study participants who had an interest in cultivating their spiritual lives tended to experience fewer hospitalizations and require less long-term care compared to peers who weren't spiritual.

Dr. Moshe Perkal

SCIENCE AND SPIRITUALITY

Dr. Moshe Perkal received his Ph.D. in chemistry from M.I.T. after graduating magna cum laude from Brandeis University. He has served as president, director, and chief scientific officer of pharmaceutical companies involved in clinical trials, FDA approval strategy, bio-pharmaceuticals, and other aspects of business development and clinical protocol design of new drugs. He has prepared over one thousand study reports which were the primary basis of approval of over five hundred generic and new drug applications. He has been published in a variety of peer-reviewed journals in the areas of bio-pharmaceuticals, chemical physics, and nuclear chemistry. Dr. Perkal and his family live in Jerusalem, where he continues to serve the international pharmaceutical industry as a consultant.

INTRODUCTION

For Torah and informed holiness to be the purpose of one's life, the Torah has to be able to withstand challenges to its claims. Torah Judaism has always responded to the challenges posed by scientific theories of contemporary cultures. And as science has advanced, reconciliation and compatibility of science and Torah has become less of an issue for the Jew who desires to practice his faith without conflict.

Science has not provided all the explanations, as yet, but not knowing why G-d did something does not prove He did not do it. The word for "world" in Hebrew is olam, which means hiding. Apparent lack of scientific knowledge or clarity about certain questions could be part of God's acknowledged policy of hiding in order to allow us free will.

The approach should be to understand Torah in its own terms by evaluating its concepts and assumptions in light of its traditions. This approach does not reject all scientific findings out of hand, it merely admits doubt of evidence that it contradicted by other reliable evidence. Just as in court a substantiated alibi overwhelms all circumstantial evidence, so with validating the Torah's account, does eyewitness testimony of the entire Jewish people at Mount Sinai cast doubt on scientific observations. However sincerely researched, scientific observations might, after all, be misleading or inaccurate.

In this century, old and cherished laws of science have been modified or abandoned. The separate principles of conservation of

matter and conservation of energy have been welded into an insep-
arable unity. The steady-state theory dared to suggest that under
certain circumstances matter is created spontaneously, ex nihilo,
something which most scientists of previous generations would have
found quite unacceptable and might have characterized as reli-
gious hypothesis.

The philosophers of science have come to realize that science's
concern is not and cannot be absolute truth. The old scientific ideal
of absolutely certain, confirmable knowledge has proven to be a
phantom. As a result, contemporary scientific statements are all
presented as tentative. And, as noted, as scientific theory advances
it becomes increasingly compatible with a spiritual life based on To-
rah.

Dr. Moshe Perkal masterfully links the compatibility of current
scientific knowledge with living a spiritual life as a Torah Jew in
the modern world.

Dr. Moshe Perkal

STORIES OF SCIENCE AND SPIRITUALITY

I grew up in the 1950s and studied science through the Ph.D., and for the last sixty years I have watched science develop. There was a time when scientists pictured themselves as investigating a great, blind machine. We humans were just cosmic accidents — a local failure of anti-septic conditions, as one wag put it. The universe, human beings included, was just atoms swirling in the void. The more scientists understood the universe, the less meaning it had. The scientific mind was confronting a giant Thing with which no communion or dialogue is possible.

Educated people picked up this picture. It seemed that science was opposed to religion and spirituality. The image of the scientist as cold, calculating, objective, detached, with no values other than finding out the truth about the universe, became a cultural icon.

The scientific picture of the world has changed greatly in

the last eighty years. In many ways the old picture is no longer viable. Discoveries within science itself are leading to a new picture of the world and of the relationship of the scientist to the world. The new picture has definite connections to the spiritual.

Here I will share with the reader two scientific stories that started within the last hundred years and are continuing to this day. The first has been told before, but some details, and some aspects of the moral have not been widely appreciated.

Once upon a time the worlds of science and philosophy agreed that the universe has no beginning. They had many reasons; here are two. First, as long as anyone could remember, the heavens have appeared to stay the same. The stars, sun, and planets go through their cycles with endless repetition. The idea of a beginning to the universe would contradict that uniform record of observation.

Second, if we try to take the idea of a beginning seriously, we are tempted to ask, "What was before the beginning?" And if we answer, "Nothing!" we are left with a giant puzzle. How can something come from nothing? We never, ever see anything like that happening in the world! Again, we would be assuming something that goes against all our experience.

More particularly, science discovered "conservation." By "conservation" science means that if you start an experiment with a certain amount of something, at the end of the experiment you will have exactly the same amount of that something. For example, it was discovered that the total of mass plus energy is conserved. So, no matter what else changed — the number of particles, their types, their motion, their energy, or anything else — the total mass-energy was always the same. That means that as far as we could tell, no mass-energy is ever created or ever lost. In other words, the universe is *closed* for mass-energy — all the mass-energy we have now was always here, and will always be here. So the mass-energy has been running around forever — there could not have been a beginning.

Then came the discovery that the stars are rushing away from each other. The universe is expanding! To call this unexpected is a gross understatement. It was a spectacular shock. The universe as a whole is changing! Contrary to all those observations that the universe does not change, here we have an astonishing observation that it does change. But more than that. This change has a very unique implication. If the universe is getting bigger, then in the past it must have been smaller. The farther back you go, the smaller it must have been. How far back can we go? Can the universe have been the size of the solar system, the size of the sun, the size of the earth, the size of New York, the size of Shea Stadium, the size of a grapefruit, the size of a peanut, the size of a grain of sand? Well, that is what they say! But this has to stop somewhere. Otherwise the universe will go down to zero size and disappear altogether! So it seems that the universe must have had a beginning sometime before we would get to zero size. That is indeed the conclusion they came to.

Now, all this time, as everyone knows, the Western religions have been teaching that the universe was created at some finite time in the past. Did science and philosophy care? Not a whit! They were convinced — dogmatically — that religion is hopelessly out of touch with the real world! And then it turned out that the real world has a beginning, just as Western religion described it!

What is the moral in this? Suppose you have a source of information that makes a prediction that you have every reason to reject. And then, against all your expectations, the prediction comes true. Do you not rethink your attitude towards the source? You may answer, how could the Bible be a source of accurate information about the physical world? And, of course, the defenders of anti-religious science will point to other cases where they "know" that religion has got it wrong. But we need to remember that one hundred years ago the teaching that the universe has a beginning was perhaps the biggest "mistake" to which they could point. If religion got that one right, how can you know the other "mistakes" will not turn out to be right?

Imagine a religious believer living one hundred years ago. When challenged by the consensus of science and philosophy against creation, what could he say? Now imagine he gave up his belief and died in 1920. What a tragedy! He gave up his belief for false science!

And now we should think further. The same book, the same tradition, that had the truth about the beginning has a lot to say about what produced the beginning and what purpose the creation is to serve. In particular, the whole of the physical world was created for a spiritual purpose. We, human beings, are a combination of the physical and the spiritual (body and soul). Our purpose lies in the way our spirit elevates the physical. If the book knew, thousands of years before science, that the universe had a beginning, then we should take seriously what it teaches about its purpose.

The second story I want to share is less well known, and very profound. Science is trying to understand how the world works. We have information — observations. We try to explain them. We concoct a theory that we think does the job. Then we test the theory — if the theory is true, then such-and-such ought to happen. We try it, we run an experiment. If such-and-such happens, that gives us some reason to trust the theory. If such-and-such does not happen, then something is wrong (with the theory, or with other assumptions, or with our calculations...).

For example, I like hard-boiled eggs. I put raw eggs in boiling water. Five minutes later they are hard-boiled. This worked well, until I was on a mountain-climbing trip. I boiled my eggs for five minutes and they came out soft-boiled! Why did that happen? Maybe it was colder on the mountain, or there was less gravity, or my clock was running fast on the mountain, or the water was agitated by the climb? Of course, you know the answer — air pressure is lower on the mountain, and water boils at a lower temperature at lower air pressure. So there was less heat in the boiling water, and so it took longer to hard-boil the eggs. And so pressure cookers were invented — if lower pressure lowers the boiling temperature of water, then raising the pressure will raise the boiling temperature. In a pressure cooker the temperature of the boiling water is much higher, so the food cooks much faster.

How do we know that this is the right theory, the right explanation? We know this because we can test the other ideas. If it were the cold on the mountain that slowed the cooking, then cooking an egg in the winter ought to take longer, and it does not. If it is gravity, then pressure cookers at the same place should not work, and they do. It is not my clock because I checked it against other clocks not on the mountain (via cell phone). It is not the agitation of the water since when I shake the water at home the cooking is not slower. That is how science works: think of a theory that will explain what you see, and then test it. But how do you think of the right theory? After all, there are so many possibilities — cold, gravity, clock, agitation. And even if there were no alternatives, why should the right factor occur to us at all? How is it that our ideas are ready to pick out the right cause?

Sometimes our ideas are not ready. Some problems take many years to solve. For example, how do diseases spread? What is lightning? How do salmon find their way back to the streams in which they hatched after traveling thousands of miles in the sea? The discovery of germs, electricity and the salmon's sense of smell took thousands of years. And some problems are still unsolved: What causes aging? How does the fertilized egg, which is a single cell, become all the different cells in our bodies? Why do blue-eyed parents sometimes have a brown-eyed child?

But very often our ideas are right on target. We have solved an immense variety of problems, and they include problems that are very far from "home." We can explain why a prism splits light into different colors, why the stars shine, and why the interior of the earth is hot. These explanations had no effect on our survival or our success when we found them. People were interested in understanding, and the ideas were there. No other creature has this kind of ability. Animals show intelligence in dealing with their environments to produce results that give them survival and success, but not beyond that. Where does our human ability for problem-solving come from?

Some will say that evolution shaped our minds to be in tune with the way the world works. Otherwise we would not have survived. But that is naive. According to evolution, many life forms have survived extremely well without any theoretical knowledge — bacteria, beetles, fish, and birds for example. Worse, the knowledge that would help us survive among the saber-toothed tigers and the food of the savannah would not help us solve the problems in the last paragraph. As we said, those problems are far from "home."

Now for the moral: Why are we right so often? We seem to have this natural, internal preference for certain kinds of theories, and when we follow that internal preference we are very often right. Why is this? Could it be that the mind is made in order to understand the world? And if so, what (or Who) made it that way? Now that book — the one that said the universe has a beginning — also says that it was created for man. And here we see that man has a special ability to understand the universe. So the picture we are building describes the universe, and man's mind, planned for human understanding.

There is a related idea. Eugene Wigner — a Nobel laureate in physics — pointed out that the applicability of abstract mathematics in physics is very strange. You have mathematicians working on completely abstract theories because those theories interest them. And later, when physicists need mathematics to describe the real world, they often find what they need already prepared. Why should the natural interests of the mathematicians be related to the way the real world is built?

Imagine, for example, we discovered that the way bees tell other bees where the flowers are is by using the rules of chess. Or that the way yeast make wine out of grape juice follows the musical scale. We would find that astonishing — why should our arbitrary games have anything to do with the way the world works? Wigner says that finding that our math works is just as astonishing.

Mark Steiner, professor of philosophy of science at the Hebrew University, takes the idea a step farther. In the most important scientific theories of the twentieth century, you find reasoning based upon the symbols used to express the laws of the theory. When a new theory was needed, scientists looked at already successful theories and tried to reproduce their symbolic style in the new theory. The similarity of symbols was considered an important factor in favor of accepting them.

Now this is truly amazing. What relationship could there by between the style of the symbols and the physical reality? Surely the symbols are conventional — the same ideas can be expressed in many different symbolic systems. And, yet, when the symbolic style was copied, the theories were successful (at least at first).

So we have more confirmation for our picture. Man's mind — even his preferences for abstract thinking, and his preferences for building symbols — are designed to give him the right ideas, the ideas needed to understand the world.

Scientists are reacting to the new picture. Some are working desperately to avoid it, to overcome it — to stay with the old model of investigating the universe as a dead machine. Some are responding to the new picture, changing their understanding of both the world and themselves. For me, the change is the most profound scientific revolution in history. It challenges us to integrate ourselves into spiritual thinkers and understand the physical world as produced by, and in service of, the spirit.

Rabbi Dr. Meir Triebitz

CREATION AND SPIRITUALITY

Rabbi Dr. Meir Triebitz attended Julliard School of Music before receiving his Ph.D. in mathematical physics from Princeton University at twenty-two years of age. He did a post-doctoral fellowship at Stanford University and then taught mathematical physics at Queens College and Stonybrook. He received rabbinical ordination before moving to Jerusalem with his family, where he teaches Judaism's thought and principles.

INTRODUCTION

Whatever one's religion or lack of it, it is an irresistible metaphor to speak of the final laws of nature in terms of the mind of God.

Steven Weinberg

The study of nature, when approached properly, can bring one to love of God. If not, the Bible tells us, "You will see the sun, the moon, and the stars, and you will turn away and bow down to them." Nature can lead a person away from God to serving idols. Whether nature is used to serve God or idolatry depends on what the person himself is looking for.

The first Soviet cosmonaut was Yuri Gargarin. He orbited the Earth one and a half times. When he returned he declared: "There is no God. Now I know it for sure. I was up there and I did not see Him." Even according to the infantile expectation of seeing a visible man on a throne in outer space, Gargarin's assertion was still ludicrously illogical. Why should Gargarin's god have been in earth orbit? Maybe the throne was too far away for him to see? Either Gargarin was a complete fool, or he was declaiming the speech required of him as a good comrade by the atheistic Soviet authorities.

In the summer of 1969, the United States sent a man to the moon. During the spectacular color telecast showing the earth from outer space, one of the astronauts read the psalm, "The heavens tell the glory of God and the firmament tells of the work of His hands." Both the Russian and the American saw the same thing, but one saw heresy and the other saw faith. Our perception of creation needs to be guided by our free hearts and minds, not by ideology.

The emphasis in Genesis on the dignity and responsibility of humankind, the summit of creation formed in the Divine image, is as valid today as at any time in history. The Sages explain the reason for humankind's having been created last: to spare us too great a task completing the creation. The Sages' understanding was that God created the world imperfect with the specific intention that humans, though created beings, would put the finishing touches on the project. But given human limitations, the work left us had to be minimal. Thus, human beings were created both greatest and last.

The pursuit of human perfection, both spiritual and otherwise, is the key to the elevation of the world. As the most significant part of creation, human beings are the part most in need of being perfected, and most able to impact the rest of the world by their own improvement. This is the moral message that faith has to offer.

Rabbi Dr. Meir Triebitz

MAN AND ETERNITY

The central debate between Jewish and Greek philosophy was focused on the "eternity" of the world. Greek philosophers, Aristotle among them, believed that the world never had a beginning in time, but rather, "always" existed. Jewish thinkers such as Maimonides asserted that the world was created from nothing, ex nihilo.

The Jews discovered the truth of the matter through their understanding of the first verse in Genesis, which reads: "In the beginning, God created heaven and earth." Although it appears to be a simple sentence, a deeper look at the verse reveals a complicated grammatical structure. The first word, *bereishis*, is commonly translated as "In the beginning," but the precise translation is actually "In the beginning *of*," as Rashi, a famous medieval commentator, points out.

The punctuation of the verse, on the other hand, as it is expressed by the musical notations which accompany the words of the text, indicates that a comma comes after the word *bereishis*, taking us back to the common translation of "In the beginning." We are left with a grammatical "tug-of-war" between meaning and punctuation.

"In the beginning of" moves the meaning of *bereishis* forward in grammar and in time, in the direction of creation. The punctuation, "In the beginning" with a comma, holds *bereishis* back and separates it from the act of creation.

Bereishis, the beginning of time, is caught between an ongoing act and a moment fixed at the edge of time, distinct and isolated from the future and disconnected from the process of creation which will occupy God for the following six days. The beginning of time, according to these interpretations, is both continuous and separated from all time.

Although it may seem like a minuscule discrepancy, there is nothing extra in the Torah, and even a comma is laden with meaning.

This paradox actually explains the idea of creation from nothing. Time can be looked at in two ways: as a separation from the past and a continuation into the future. The determining factor is perspective, or which way you are looking at it. Looking backwards from the future into the past, time seems natural and continuous and, when viewed only from this perspective, it may seem that time extends back into the past indefinitely. On the other hand, if your perspective is positioned at the moment of creation, then there is only the future and no past at all. In that case, the first moment must have a mark of distinction from all that comes after it, which is indicated by the comma in the text.

This two-sided interpretation of time ultimately leads us to two distinct interpretations of God: one as God the Creator, who puts nature into motion, and the second as God who stands apart and separate from nature. There are two names for these true aspects of God: *Elokim* and *Yud-kei-vav-kei*.

Greek philosophy only recognizes God as *Elokim*. They see God as the Creator of the world but with no other function. They see God as being the same as His creation, and they recognize God as eternal. From here comes the belief that His creation is also eternal. God is seen as the God of nature and can't be separated from it or transcend it.

Jewish thinking recognizes another aspect of God along with this. True, God is the Creator, but He also existed before He created the world. This paradox is the cornerstone of the Jewish philosophy of creation and the relationship of God to the created world. The truth emerges from the meaning and grammar of the first verse in Genesis. Creation ex nihilo is not a spontaneous event. It is a manifestation of God's word. Only God's Divine command can establish creation. A conception of God as creating but not commanding excludes part of the process.

Morality Crisis

Modernization has brought in its wake a serious decline in morality. Ever since a British philosopher named David Hume demonstrated that one cannot derive an "ought" from an "is," the scientific view of the world, which describes the "is," has stopped producing moral concepts.

The central event of history from which this moral crisis emerged was the Holocaust. The very fact that the elimination of an entire people was conceived and almost perfectly executed by the most advanced scientific and cultural people on earth is now permanently embedded in the human consciousness as the natural consequence of the lowering of morality and the lack of meaning which afflicts mankind. While attempts have been made to create a new moral order composed of values not traditional for the West (new-age, Eastern spirituality), or to recover pre-modern worldviews (MacIntyre), the basis for a moral imperative still remains elusive and tenuous, especially in view of the scientific and technological onslaught of the modern world.

This morality crisis in the modern world has its roots in the Greek conception of creation which was outlined previously. Reducing God to mere nature obscures reality. Perceiving God as dependent on His creation reduces Him to a scientific event which cannot command moral authority. Hume's assertion that one cannot derive an "ought" from an "is" is simply a restatement of the Greek fallacy that God Himself is nothing but an "is." While man could conjure up his own moral imperatives, they would never actually be rooted in objective reality. While the Greeks surely developed systems of moral reasoning and philosophies about God, these were eventually washed away by man's increasingly scientific worldviews. As that which "is" became more and more scientifically exact and rigorous, morality fell away because it was proven unnecessary, irrelevant, and unscientific.

Creation from Nothing

Let's return to Genesis. We said before that the Bible contains two names for God: *Elokim* and *Yud-kei-vav-kei*. The story of creation is actually recorded twice in Genesis. In the first accounting in chapter 1, God's name appears only as *Elokim*. In the second telling in chapter 2, both names of God appear, *Elokim* and *Yud-kei-vav-kei*.

Chapter 1 reads:

> *Elokim* said, "Let us make man with our image and likeness..." *Elokim* thus created man with His image. In the image of *Elokim* He created him; male and female He created them. *Elokim* blessed them. *Elokim*

said to them, "Be fertile and become many. Fill the land and conquer it. Dominate the fish of the sea, the birds of the sky, and every beast that walks the land."

In this version of creation, the man and the woman are created simultaneously. Man is not alone at any time. He always co-exists with his female partner.

In chapter 2, we are given an entirely different account of the creation of the first woman. Chapter 2 reads:

> *Yud-kei-vav-kei Elokim* said, "It is not good that man be alone. I will make a compatible helper for him... *Yud-kei-vav-kei Elokim* then made man fall into a deep sleep, and he slept. He took one of his ribs and closed the flesh in its place. *Yud-kei-vav-kei Elokim* built the rib that He took from the man into a woman, and He brought her to the man. Man said, "Now this is bone from my bones and flesh from my flesh. She shall be called woman because she was taken from man." A man shall therefore leave his father and mother and be united with his wife, and they shall become one flesh.

In this second account of creation, man is created alone, and woman is created as a separate entity who unites with man later on.

In the first version, having been created together with woman, man never experiences solitude. He has no need to encounter and relate to another human being. He is oblivious to others. Here, despite the creation of both man and woman together, only the name of *Elokim* is used.

In the second accounting of creation, man is forced to confront his solitude. Human relationships are therefore born in the second account, whereas they were superfluous, even non-existent, in the first. In this version, both terms for God, *Yud-kei-vav-kei* and *Elokim*, are used. What are these names and their specific usages coming to teach us?

Let's return to the first verse in Genesis and our discussion. The first verse reads, on the surface, "In the beginning, God created heaven and earth."

Or, more precisely, *Elokim* created heaven and earth.

We noted that the term used for creation, *bereishis*, and its punctuation brought us to the truth of creation from nothing. The concept is embedded into the verse and remains hidden beneath the surface structure of the text. The idea of creation ex nihilo transcends the physical world and consists of God's word and command. Man encounters not only a world in progress in space and time, but also the spoken word of God as He relates to man through His word. This begins in the first chapter with the command to be fertile and become many and fill (subdue) the land. But this is only vis-à-vis physical creation. It doesn't contain a truly moral dimension because man is created "complete," without need for any other human being. This is the *Elokim* aspect.

Only in the second account of creation, when man is created alone and part of himself is extracted to be created as a woman to be rejoined to him, only then can man encounter another person and be brought into a relationship which transcends creation. Creation has to be dislodged, broken, and then reconstituted in a larger context in order for man to establish a relationship with another human being. It is therefore in this second account of creation that the term *Yud-kei-vav-kei* is joined to the term *Elokim*, for the encounter with woman is an expression of creation ex nihilo through the name *Yud-kei-vav-kei*. Man and woman both reflect and are an actual outcome of the two names of God. This duality is the very essence of creation ex nihilo.

This is the source of morality in Jewish thought. Morality is born out of the concept of creation ex nihilo. Creation is both an "ought" and an "is," both necessary components born out of God's role as both a Creator and He who has an ongoing relationship with man.

A Complete Life

The Bible's two accounts of creation present two relationships between man and God.

1. Man's relationship with God as the Source of Creation.

2. Man's relationship with God as the Source of moral imperative.

In the first relationship, man confronts the world in all its dazzling and awesome scientific beauty. The complexity and depth of nature evokes within man a consciousness of spirituality which sees its source in the Divine act of Creation. The second relationship confronts man with that other who evokes within man a consciousness of Divine law and justice. By its very nature, this second relationship beckons to man to heed God's call to the Divine moral imperative.

The complete life must contain both relationships, for they both compliment and enhance each other. Only the totality of scientific and moral consciousness can be brought to bear on man's spiritual life, in his quest for human and hence Divine perfection.

Rabbi Berel Wein

ETHICAL LIVING

Rabbi Berel Wein, *the founder and director of the Destiny Foundation since 1996, has for over twenty years been identified with the popularization of Jewish history through world-wide lectures, audiotapes, books, weekend programs, and most recently educational tours and documentary films. Rabbi Wein is a graduate of the Hebrew Theological College, and Roosevelt College in Chicago. He received his Juris Doctor Degree from DePaul University Law School and a Doctor of Hebrew Letters from Hebrew Theological College. Rabbi Wein was a practicing lawyer for a number of years. Rabbi Wein authored a trilogy on Jewish history, comprised of* Triumph of Survival, the Story of the Jews in the Modern Era; Herald of Destiny, the Medieval Era; *and* Echoes of Glory, the Classical Era, *all of which have received popular and critical acclaim. Rabbi Wein was the recipient of the Educator of the Year Award from the Covenant Foundation in 1993. He and his wife now make their home in Jerusalem.*

INTRODUCTION

Every act that a Jew performs, whether in the workplace, while driving, or when paying taxes, needs ethical guidelines. Our world has undergone tremendous technological changes, but the issues stay the same — egotism, jealousy, greed, bribery, corruption. People want to do the right thing, but they no longer have an inner moral compass.

Our Torah teaches us that the most important tasks in the material world are precisely those that help create an abode for sanctity. Judaism's ethical laws are predicated on respect for human dignity, and honesty is a basic Jewish value. This certainly applies to financial matters, which play such an important part of our lives. Judaism considers the earning of money as a constructive economic activity. Even though our economic success, or lack thereof, is determined by God, we have to make an effort to do our best within what is permissible. Increased effort may increase profit, but only in sanctioned activity. If money is earned in a forbidden activity by unjust enrichment, one ultimately will have to pay dearly for the transgression. As Rabbi Hillel said, "Not all those who increase their wealth are wise."

The Torah forbids deceiving any human being. This is true even if no one suffers a loss, because not only are the laws there to protect rightful owners, but to guarantee our own ethical behavior. We are forbidden to use high-pressure tactics to force another person into a business deal and even to plan such deals, even if the sec-

ond party eventually consents and receives proper payment. Truth in advertising requires unequivocally that one may not misrepresent a product in terms of nature or origin and that one must fully disclose all aspects of the product not immediately obvious, unless the hidden features improve it or the defects are accessible and customers always inspect the product. This, of course, does not remove responsibility from the consumers to be knowledgeable about market practices and take reasonable precautions, as any aware and astute person would.

Another reason for honesty is that one must walk in God's ways. Just as God is truthful, so truthfulness and godliness cannot be separated. The difficulties involved in maintaining a high level of honesty are challenging. To maintain a moral life requires permanent alertness, constant choice, and uninterrupted struggle. The immediate reward is the satisfaction of the life you have created for yourself.

Success in earning a living is a praiseworthy achievement, but the striving must be used to affirm a Jew's godly mission. The dictates of ethical business are not to make us love money, but rather to enable us to turn our success in this world into a holy experience.

The Torah obligates using one's financial resources for Divine service: "And you shall love the Lord your God...with all your soul and with all your resources." Rabbi Akiva was asked if in addition to giving up one's life, one must also be commanded to give up all his money for love of God. He replied that there are some people whose money is more important to them than life.

Rabbi Berel Wein, a pulpit rabbi with the responsibility to warn Jews of the potential spiritual dangers of materialism, comments on the proper perspective in spending money and the disastrous effects of those who overemphasize materialism in their daily lives. God rests His presence not necessarily where there is wealth, but where there is righteousness.

The prophets of old gave admonition to the Jewish people to correct their failures. The prophets wrote their criticisms larger than life in order to impress on the Jewish people the proper path to follow. Rabbi Wein follows in their footsteps, applying sublime ethical Jewish norms to contemporary Jewish society, emphasizing shortcoming as a means to stimulating improvement. Of course, the full picture includes myriad inspiring ethical successes. As he writes at the end of this article, "In our generation all Jews are heroes. Anyone still standing in the shadow of Auschwitz who proclaims 'Ivri anochi — I am a Jew' is to be admired, complimented, and aided."

But with admiration and compliment must go self-criticism and scrutiny and the willingness to try to be better.

Rabbi Berel Wein

THE JEW IN THE LAND
OF PLENTY

There is one who waxes wealthy and possesses nothing,
and one who is impoverished and has great wealth.

Mishlei 13:7
(according to the translation of the Malbim)

Jewish history is replete with differing problems, paradoxes, and challenges. But the basic problem that faces every generation is how to remain truly Jewish in an overwhelmingly non-Jewish world. The Torah itself addresses this problem: "How do these nations worship their gods? Let me also do likewise!" And the story of the Jewish people in their long exile is again one of that struggle to remain uniquely Jewish in spite of the pressures of an alien, encroaching, and different world.

As long as the world was openly hostile to the Jew, as in much of Europe during the Middle Ages, then, perversely, it was easier for Jews to remain thoroughly Jewish. As the ghetto walls began to fall in the eighteenth and nineteenth centuries, however, the problem of being Jewish became acute once again, and this still is the greatest problem facing American Orthodox Jewry. We are attempting to live a life that conforms to Torah and halachah (Jewish law) while living and participating in a society whose value system is completely inimical to the value system implicit in halachah. We lead lives that at least superficially conform to the requirements of halachah, but what about the ethical values of our Orthodox society and its priorities? Are we truly Jewish?

Attributed to Rabbi S. R. Hirsch, famed Rav of Frankfurt-am-Main until his passing one hundred years ago, is a comment that still rings true in late twenty-first-century America. "The Marranos of Spain were goyim on the outside and Jews on the inside. My Jews are reverse Marranos." The problem facing American Orthodoxy is that no matter how *frum* we appear on the outside, our inside may reflect the American way of life. Some of us think as the general society thinks, its value system is ours, its goals are ours, and its measures of success are definitive for us as well. It is difficult to be part of a halachic society that lives a life system that for some mocks halachic Jewish values.

"Religion" without Ethics

According to the Midrash, Esau fooled his father, Isaac, while mocking him by asking him *she'eilos* (halachic questions). "How does one give the tithe from straw?" That is a halachic question; it has a halachic answer and Isaac undoubtedly did so answer Esau, giving his son the benefit of the doubt. But the Rabbis, from the perspective of later millennia, having seen what became of Esau and his descendants, saw in that halachic *she'eilah* a mockery of all that Jewish life stands for.

It brings to mind the story of the man about to embark on a ten-day cruise on *erev* Pesach who frantically calls his Rav. "I've checked out the matzos and the food, and it's all *mehadrin*. But the ship will be sailing in international waters, and there will be casino gambling on board. Do they have to provide all new gambling chips for Pesach?" Such people ask all sorts of nitty-gritty questions regarding kashrus, and miss the whole point of leading a Torah life, fulfilling the awful description of the Ramban of being a *naval*, a disgusting person, while remaining somehow within the parameters of Torah law.

This bitterly amusing anecdote is symptomatic of the failures of our society, where the federal prisons of our country provide Jewish inmates with strictly kosher food on a regular basis. When the author headed the kashrus department of the OU, a warden called to review his Pesach order. After Pesach, the OU received a blistering letter of criticism from one of the inmates at that prison, who demanded a particular brand of coffee for Pesach and was upset by the "inadequacy" of the recommended brand.

The element of shame has disappeared from some in our Jewish society, just as it has disappeared from the general society. Exposure has become one of the risks of the game: If one gets caught, then one gets caught. If not, then one has won the game and successfully beaten the odds; forget about the felony. These are the rules of certain elements within contemporary Jewish society; it is not a question of right or wrong — or sanctifying or blaspheming God's name — only whether the potential gain is worth the risk. They are more concerned with *"frum"* coffee than with the true ethics of being a halachically observant person.

A "Thing-Centered" Society

The Midrash describes the generation of the Tower of Babel in ways that bear some resemblance to ours. They were concerned with things, but not with people. If a brick fell from the tower and was smashed, they mourned the loss; but if a human being fell, that was all part of the risk associated with technological progress. Construction projects, space-shuttle programs, new highway techniques, all are achieved at the cost of the quality of human life. Society generally is more interested in things — furniture, objets d'art, foreign sports cars — than in people, especially people who are different from the norm. This attitude is found in Jewish America, as well. Materialism and conspicuous consumption of goods destroy the fabric of a life consistent with Torah values and halachic principles. At times, too much becomes too little and more is definitely less. The test of affluence is a difficult one to pass.

God has granted us plenty, perhaps because of the terrible tragedies of the previous generation — like a spoiled child, born after a terrible tragedy in a family. So has God granted us many things that some Jews don't quite know how to deal with: great material wealth and new opportunities, a resurgence of Torah study and traditional life, a Jewish state in the Land of Israel. Their successes have overwhelmed them. They are unable to place them into historic perspective and thus deal with them in an optimum fashion.

For many years, a Shabbos afternoon "Mishnah Club" met in my house for a number of boys aged five to twelve. By year's end, my closet would house a collection of coats, gloves, scarves, and ties — many with designer labels, costing a great deal of money. (When I was young, if I lost my coat...there would not be a second coat.) Yet no one called to ask about a missing coat. A child who loses his coat will, as a matter of right and course, receive another one. No wonder there is no respect for clothing among some of our children... A society that values things over people, eventually respects neither.

Thing versus Substance

This thing-centered attitude has spilled over into the observance of mitzvos to the point that some measure the enhancement of mitzvah performance (*hiddur mitzvah*) primarily in terms of monetary costs. For them, this *hiddur* today is a thinly-disguised form of social one-upmanship. The evil inclination has entered the mitzvah business. Indoor removable sukkah-rooms; hundred-dollar *esrogim* encased in luxurious boxes; more expensive, though not necessarily more reliable, kosher products; enormously expensive Sabbath clothes...all are the vogue. But unfortunately, the mitzvah ethic is sometimes lost in the *hiddur* wrapping.

A number of years ago, a certain Rav in Jerusalem was observed by a well-known writer purchasing an *esrog* before Sukkos. The writer then saw the Rav on Sukkos morning without *lulav* or *esrog*. "What happened to your *esrog*?" he asked.

The Rav answered, "I'll tell you, but only if you do not write of it until after my death."

Next door to him lived a Jew with a very short temper who frequently beat his children for minor infractions of home rules. On Sukkos morning, the Rav awoke early to hear weeping from the balcony next door. His neighbor's daughter had been holding her father's *esrog* and had inadvertently dropped it, breaking off the top piece and rendering it unusable and unfit for the mitzvah. The girl was in tears, fully anticipating her father's wrath. The Rav reached over, placed his *esrog* in his neighbor's *esrog* box, and told her to tell her father that he, the Rav, had examined the neighbor's *esrog* and had decided that the new *esrog* was more proper for him. And the Rav took away the broken *esrog*. The writer correctly titled the story, when he finally wrote it, "*Hiddur Mitzvah*." It reflects a unique concept, an authentic Jewish value system of how to deal with halachic problems. This concept should be applied in our society.

The Values in Career Choices

Living a life guided by the way things seem rather than by their inner content, stressing things over values, can lead a person to opt for an unfortunate career. Now, choice of career may seem to be a "neutral area," but it can touch on some fundamental problems of halachah and of basic values. Not every career is for every Jewish boy, and certainly not for every Jewish girl. Because of our success in achieving equal opportunity in the professional world and the marketplace, we are dealing with a generation in which some see no limits to their horizons. One can, without undue penalty, wear a *kippah*, eat kosher food, and be fully Sabbath and Yom Tov observant in the medical centers, the boardrooms of major corporations, the legal centers, and the highest levels of government in our country. But the price of "making it" in our world is not small.

The Rabbis' admonition to engage in a career that is "light and clean" (*umanus kallah u'nekiyah*) is always relevant. Today people immediately think in terms of computers. They may be right, but one could challenge that. Basically a light and clean career is one that will permit a person to come home at a reasonable hour, and enable them to spend time with family, children, synagogue, and Torah.

The archetypal Jewish mother wants her son to be (at least) a lawyer. Today, your average yeshivah graduate can make it through law school, pass the bar, and go on to the most prestigious law firms in the country, at no recognizable cost to his *Yiddishkeit*. But as a successful lawyer, he will not see his children awake from one Shabbos to the next. (I speak from experience; I was a lawyer for nine years before becoming a full-time Rabbi.) If a lawyer wants to "make it," he has to leave the house at six in the morning and attend appointments with clients at ten at night. One is not paid $100,000 per year as an entering lawyer in a Park Avenue law firm and expect to work normal hours or have a normal family life. Law is not light and clean.

The yeshivah where I am the principal, certainly not exceptional in this regard, has a number of orphans with living parents. The father works, the mother works, and the house is empty — physically, psychologically, educationally, spiritually — deafeningly empty. The child would be better served to come home to a more modest physical environment, endowed with a presence of people of tradition and warmth and care and interest and love. The largest industry in our suburban community is child care — babysitting! No one is home.

Is it worth it? I doubt it.

Of Professions, Purposes, and Destiny

The individual's choice of profession and career is vital to the future of the Jewish people and the fulfillment of our cosmic purpose. The mother of one of my students complained that her son decided to study Torah in Israel for a year or two after graduation from *mesivta* high school. Her son would "lose a year," which he would need later in his medical education.

I dared ask her the unspeakable question: "Why must he be a doctor?"

She answered, "I don't understand you. He may discover the cure for cancer. Do you want to prevent that?"

My answer wasn't easy for her to swallow. It opened up for her a different dimension in world perspective.

God has created a great and varied world. There are over four billion non-Jews in the world. We don't have to do everything in the world by ourselves. The Jews are not obligated to supply all of the doctors, lawyers, judges, corporate raiders, real-estate developers, and entrepreneurs of this world. The Jews are, however, obligated to be the Jewish people, with all the moral and ethical obligations that this implies. We should have no objection to an Italian or an Irishman or a Black or a Hispanic discovering the cure for cancer. But Torah, halachah, Jewish ethics, and eternal value systems are the primary Jewish agenda, both nationally and individually. What I can do, only I can do; our role in the world is therefore very exclusive. Hence, the choice of a light and clean career is a crucial one. If the choice is not directed at propagating Jewish values, it should at least honor those values and permit ample time for their pursuit.

"*Ivri Anochi* — I Am a Jew"

Although I have some points for consideration to bring improvement in the Jewish people, my general view of the Jewish people, especially in our generation, is that all Jews are heroes. Anyone still standing in the shadow of Auschwitz who proclaims "*Ivri anochi* — I am a Jew" is to be admired, complimented, and aided. We are the only Jewish people around, and the Lord apparently is still willing to deal with us on His usual exact, demanding, and intimate terms. Therefore, to the extent that we can address our problems realistically and put ourselves in the proper perspective of Jewish historical tradition vis-à-vis the non-halachic society in which we live, will we be able to continue to see the supremacy of halachic thought and values in our lives and continue to be authentically Jewish in the full sense of the term.

Dr. Moshe Kaplan

Epilogue

A COMPLETE MAN

Remembering My Rebbe

As the Jewish nation journeyed from Egypt through the desert to Israel, two *aronot* (boxes) led their way. Bystanders were astonished. Why were these boxes given such prominence? What were in these boxes? The Jews responded that in one box was God's Torah and in the second box were the bones of Joseph, our former leader. The bystanders were now more perplexed. Why do the bones of flesh and blood deserve such respect? Certainly they cannot be considered of equal importance to God's Torah. The Jews replied succinctly: Joseph's box is of crucial importance because "He expressed all that was written in the Torah" (*Sotah* 13b).

The nations were amazed, but to the Jews, the value of Joseph's bones was axiomatic. The path to completion can begin with studying ideas, but can only continue when we experience the greatness of the ideas chiseled out in the daily lives of the righteous. As a nation, we have always understood these dual sources of greatness: the theoretical word and the practical deeds of the righteous. Words come to life when we experience them. One can discuss love and heroism, but the concepts are only shadows of existence until we fall in love or rise to heroism. The experiential world expresses a depth and energy that tugs at our entire being in a way that words do not.

Great people show that ideas are more powerful and noble in action than they appear on a flat page of print. In this book I have sought to help you relate to the truth and relevance of our Jewish heritage, but I would be remiss not to share with you a second part of our heritage. Other nations pride themselves on their creations in concrete and steel. Our nation is ennobled by unique creations in flesh and blood — the creation of complete men, the creation of *tzaddikim* (righteous people). This is our unique gift to the history of man.

Meeting such a person changed my life. Having been raised with princes and presidents, never had I met a person as complete and uplifting as my Rebbe, HaGaon HaRav Chaim Kreiswirth, *zt"l*, the Chief Rabbi of Antwerp, Belgium. What made his greatness unique? Rav Yehudah HaLevi in his classic book, the *Kuzari*, asks who is a righteous person? How can we identify him? Is it wisdom? Asceticism? What sets him apart? Rav Yehudah HaLevi answers that a righteous person is like a ruler who gives to each part of his kingdom its proper due. All the potential of the kingdom must be expressed for the king to be a distinguished ruler. Similarly, to be a righteous person one must express his righteousness in all the dimensions that make us human. My book has sought to express the multiple facets that make up a good, complete Jewish life. My Rebbe lived and allowed me to experience this Jewish ideal.

Rav Chaim was an intellectual genius with a phenomenal memory: deep, broad, and creative. He knew the length and breadth of the sea of the Talmud. At age twenty he was already a senior instructor in the most prominent rabbinic institution of Poland, Yeshivas Chachmei Lublin. But he was not just a great scholar; he was also an active educator who invested much time and energy in his students' spiritual growth. From Poland to Chicago to Antwerp he raised up his students to become leaders in their own right.

This would be a full-time profession for many a great man. However, Rav Chaim's vision of man inspired him to expand beyond the study hall and he also took upon himself the responsibilities of the broader community. He became the chief rabbi of the city of Antwerp. For forty years the concerns of his entire community became his personal concerns. But his heart and soul were still not satisfied, as there was so much more that a Jew could do. The indigent, the widowed, and the orphans in the land of Israel roused him to action. He traveled the world to collect money to help these troubled souls. He knew no rest in his efforts to help them and enable them to overcome their difficulties. Tens of millions of dollars were gathered by him humbly, quietly, and modestly to aid the less fortunate. He did not limit himself to financial assistance but he also sought to provide emotional support and assistance to these needy people. He raised money by the thousands, but loved people one at a time.

His communal obligations greatly diminished the personal time available for his precious and beloved Torah study, but he happily accepted this sacrifice. He was once asked why he had not composed a book of his insights into the Torah. The Rav responded he had written a very special book. He then pulled out his charity ledger with the names of widows and orphans for whom he had raised money. "Here is my book. This happy orphan and this consoled widow. It is this book that I will take with me to show God when I pass on."

All this he did with good character and a sense of humor that was unique. I remember a few years before he passed away, Rav Chaim had a mini-stroke. He was hospitalized and under close medical supervision. The family decided that it would be advisable to have someone with him day and night in the hospital. I was a close student and also a doctor so I had the honor of the night shift. By the third night of dozing in a hospital chair I was exhausted, and I fell asleep during my shift. At about 4 a.m. Rav Chaim woke in pain from his sleep, but greeted me with a witty comment: "I am awake and my doctor is sleeping." After that, no matter how challenging life has become, I have always tried to maintain my sense of humor.

Never have I met a person who so embodied all the facets that make one a great human being as my spiritual mentor, HaGaon HaRav Chaim Kreiswirth, *zt"l*. For eighteen years I had the special privilege of developing a close personal relationship with him. His love and devotion made me feel like the world was created for me. He helped me grow and develop.

Like the Jews in the desert we all need two boxes to help us develop our potential. This book is meant to be a first step, but the next is yours. Please find yourself a role model, a mentor, a Rebbe. Connect yourself to the Jewish community so you can experience your unique Jewish greatness: the ability to create a complete human being.

The words of Torah and the righteousness of Rav Chaim have given me a fuller life. It is my prayer that you too should experience this growth and development. At joyous significant occasions we Jews lift our cups of wine and bless each other with *L'chayim* — to life. Rav Chaim was a constant "*l'chayim*" to all who knew him. We became more complete, more fulfilled, happier, and more alive from knowing him. I wanted to share that blessing with you in this short book. So let me close by wishing you a *l'chayim* — may you grow and create a life filled with Torah joys and completion.

And if you would like to contact the person in your area who could tell you more, e-mail me at rebirth613@hotmail.com.